GOD'S
MIGHTY
PROPHETS

GOD'S
MIGHTY
PROPHETS

Compiled by Eugene Carvalho

God's Mighty Prophets

Copyright © 2019 by Eugene Carvalho

ISBN: 9781091809772

Printed in the United States of America

To the Body of Christ.
May this compilation bless you richly!
With love…

TABLE OF CONTENTS

PURPOSE AND ACKNOWLEDGEMENTS

The infallible Word of God for faith and conduct informs us that the Holy Spirit gives gifts to men and women of the Body of Christ. It states: "the gifts edify the body for the building up of the saints" (Eph. 4:12). I hope the talents and gifts the Lord has given me will be a blessing to someone else through the reading of this compilation.

I am grateful for the love I have received from family members, especially my wife Mercedes Carvalho. I am also grateful for the knowledge, wisdom and love of many pastors, teachers, and saints that the Lord has used to bless me. Lastly, I must not forget a special thank you to my friend Kathryn Regan for proofreading this material.

Chapter One

GOD'S MIGHTY PROPHETS

The office of the prophet was not just for Old Testament times. The New Testament informs us, "And He gave some as apostles, and some as prophets, and some as evangelists, and some as pastors and teachers, for the equipping of the saints for the work of service, to the building up of the body of Christ; until we all attain to the unity of the faith, and of the knowledge of the Son of God, to a mature man, to the measure of the stature which belongs to the fullness of Christ" (Eph. 4:11-13). So we see Jesus gave the gift of prophecy to individuals.

It's important to understand how God uses a prophet. They not only predict the future but are used in other ways as well. One way is to show that God is God. He demonstrated His power through the prophets. They are also used by God to proclaim his word.

At times prophecy warns individuals about their actions. Other times prophecy can be used to encourage individuals when their circumstances appear dreadful.

Like the gift of prophecy, tongues that are interpreted have the effect of encouraging and blessing the church to love and serve God more deeply and effectively. However, Paul writes and states, "Pursue love, yet desire earnestly spiritual gifts, but especially that you may prophesy" (1 Cor. 14:1).

We are able to draw conclusions and understand the office of the prophet is needed and valued even to this day. We live in the midst of a crooked and perverse generation. Jesus is coming back soon. We must heed the cry of the prophets of old along with the prophets of this present age and be on guard. I remember some of the last words spoken in the Bible by my favorite prophet, Jesus Christ. He said, "Behold, I am coming quickly, and My reward is with Me, to render to every man according to what he has done. I am the Alpha and the Omega, the first and the last, the beginning and the end" (Rev. 22:12-13).

With that being said, let us investigate a vast array of scriptures from the Old and New Testament that discuss the God's prophets. They will give you fresh revelation and insight, build your faith, and be a blessing to you.

Chapter Two

PROPHETS IN THE OLD TESTAMENT

IN THE BOOK OF GENESIS

Restore the Man's Wife, For He is a Prophet

"Now Abraham journeyed from there toward the land of the Negev, and settled between Kadesh and Shur; then he sojourned in Gerar. And Abraham said of Sarah his wife, 'She is my sister.' So Abimelech king of Gerar sent and took Sarah. But God came to Abimelech in a dream of the night, and said to him, 'Behold, you are a dead man because of the woman whom you have taken, for she is married.' Now Abimelech had not come near her; and he said, 'Lord, wilt Thou slay a nation, even though blameless? Did he not himself say to me, "She is my sister"? And she herself said, "He is my brother." In the integrity of my heart and the innocence of my hands I have done this.' Then God said to him in the dream, 'Yes, I know that in the integrity of your heart you have done this, and I also kept you from sinning against Me; therefore I did not let you touch her. Now therefore, restore the man's wife, for he is a prophet, and he will pray for you, and you will live. But if you do not restore her, know that you shall surely die, you and all who are yours"' (Ge. 20:1-7).

Chapter Two

IN THE BOOK OF EXODUS

Moses Your Brother Aaron Shall Be Your Prophet

"Then the Lord said to Moses, 'See, I make you as God to Pharaoh, and your brother Aaron shall be your prophet. You shall speak all that I command you, and your brother Aaron shall speak to Pharaoh that he let the sons of Israel go out of his land. But I will harden Pharaoh's heart that I may multiply My signs and My wonders in the land of Egypt. When Pharaoh will not listen to you, then I will lay My hand on Egypt, and bring out My hosts, My people the sons of Israel, from the land of Egypt by great judgments. And the Egyptians shall know that I am the Lord, when I stretch out My hand on Egypt and bring out the sons of Israel from their midst.' So Moses and Aaron did it; as the Lord commanded them, thus they did. And Moses was eighty years old and Aaron eighty-three, when they spoke to Pharaoh" (Ex. 7:1-7).

IN THE BOOK OF NUMBERS

If There Is a Prophet Among You

"Then Miriam and Aaron spoke against Moses because of the Cushite woman whom he had married (for he had married a Cushite woman); and they said, 'Has the Lord indeed spoken only through Moses? Has He not spoken through us as well?' And the Lord heard it. (Now the man Moses was very humble, more than any man who was on the face of the earth.) And suddenly the Lord said to Moses and

Aaron and to Miriam, 'You three come out to the tent of meeting.' So the three of them came out. Then the Lord came down in a pillar of cloud and stood at the doorway of the tent, and He called Aaron and Miriam. When they had both come forward, He said, 'Hear now My words: If there is a prophet among you, I, the Lord, shall make Myself known to him in a vision. I shall speak with him in a dream. Not so, with My servant Moses, He is faithful in all My household; With him I speak mouth to mouth, Even openly, and not in dark sayings, And he beholds the form of the Lord. Why then were you not afraid to speak against My servant, against Moses?'" (Nu. 12:1-8).

IN THE BOOK OF DEUTERONOMY

A Prophet or a Dreamer of Dreams

"If a prophet or a dreamer of dreams arises among you and gives you a sign or a wonder, and the sign or the wonder comes true, concerning which he spoke to you, saying, 'Let us go after other gods (whom you have not known) and let us serve them,' you shall not listen to the words of that prophet or that dreamer of dreams; for the Lord your God is testing you to find out if you love the Lord your God with all your heart and with all your soul. You shall follow the Lord your God and fear Him; and you shall keep His commandments, listen to His voice, serve Him, and cling to Him. But that prophet or that dreamer of dreams shall be put to death, because he has counseled rebellion against the Lord your God who brought you from the land of Egypt and redeemed you from the house of slavery, to seduce you from the way in which the Lord your God commanded you to walk. So you shall purge the evil from among you" (Dt. 13:1-5).

God Will Raise Up for You a Prophet

"The Lord your God will raise up for you a prophet like me from among you, from your countrymen, you shall listen to him. This is according to all that you asked of the Lord your God in Horeb on the day of the assembly, saying, 'Let me not hear again the voice of the Lord my God, let me not see this great fire anymore, lest I die.' And the Lord said to me, 'They have spoken well. I will raise up a prophet from among their countrymen like you, and I will put My words in his mouth, and he shall speak to them all that I command him. And it shall come about that whoever will not listen to My words which he shall speak in My name, I Myself will require it of him. But the prophet who shall speak a word presumptuously in My name which I have not commanded him to speak, or which he shall speak in the name of other gods, that prophet shall die. And you may say in your heart, 'How shall we know the word which the Lord has not spoken?' When a prophet speaks in the name of the Lord, if the thing does not come about or come true, that is the thing which the Lord has not spoken. The prophet has spoken it presumptuously; you shall not be afraid of him" (Dt. 18:15-22).

Chapter Two

No Prophet Has Risen in Israel Like Moses

"Now Joshua the son of Nun was filled with the spirit of wisdom, for Moses had laid his hands on him; and the sons of Israel listened to him and did as the Lord had commanded Moses. Since then no prophet has risen in Israel like Moses, whom the Lord knew face to face, for all the signs and wonders which the Lord sent him to perform in the land of Egypt against Pharaoh, all his servants, and all his land, and for all the mighty power and for all the great terror which Moses performed in the sight of all Israel" (Dt. 34:9-12).

IN THE BOOK OF JUDGES

The Lord Sent a Prophet to the Sons of Israel

"Now it came about when the sons of Israel cried to the Lord on account of Midian, that the Lord sent a prophet to the sons of Israel, and he said to them, 'Thus says the Lord, the God of Israel, "It was I who brought you up from Egypt, and brought you out from the house of slavery. And I delivered you from the hands of the Egyptians and from the hands of all your oppressors, and dispossessed them before you and gave you their land, and I said to you, 'I am the Lord your God; you shall not fear the gods of the Amorites in whose land you live. But you have not obeyed Me""'" (Jdg. 6:7-10).

Chapter Two

IN THE BOOK OF 1 SAMUEL

Samuel was Confirmed as a Prophet of the Lord

"Thus Samuel grew and the Lord was with him and let none of his words fail. And all Israel from Dan even to Beersheba knew that Samuel was confirmed as a prophet of the Lord. And the Lord appeared again at Shiloh, because the Lord revealed Himself to Samuel at Shiloh by the word of the Lord" (1Sa. 3:19-21).

He Who is Called a Prophet Now was Formerly Called a Seer

"When they came to the land of Zuph, Saul said to his servant who was with him, 'Come, and let us return, lest my father cease to be concerned about the donkeys and become anxious for us.' And he said to him, 'Behold now, there is a man of God in this city, and the man is held in honor; all that he says surely comes true. Now let us go there, perhaps he can tell us about our journey on which we have set out.' Then Saul said to his servant, 'But behold, if we go, what shall we bring the man? For the bread is gone from our sack and there is no present to bring to the man of God. What do we have?' And the servant answered Saul again and said, 'Behold, I have in my hand a fourth of a shekel of silver; I will give it to the man of God and he will tell us our way.' (Formerly in Israel, when a man went to inquire of God, he used to say, 'Come, and let us go to the seer'; for he who is called a prophet now was formerly called a seer.) Then Saul said to his servant,

'Well said; come, let us go.' So they went to the city where the man of God was" (1Sa. 9:5-10).

The Prophet Gad Informed David

"And David went from there to Mizpah of Moab; and he said to the king of Moab, 'Please let my father and my mother come and stay with you until I know what God will do for me.' Then he left them with the king of Moab; and they stayed with him all the time that David was in the stronghold. And the prophet Gad said to David, 'Do not stay in the stronghold; depart, and go into the land of Judah.' So David departed and went into the forest of Hereth" (1Sa. 22:3-5).

IN THE BOOK OF 2 SAMUEL

The King Said to Nathan the Prophet

"Now it came about when the king lived in his house, and the Lord had given him rest on every side from all his enemies, that the king said to Nathan the prophet, 'See now, I dwell in a house of cedar, but the ark of God dwells within tent curtains.' And Nathan said to the king, 'Go, do all that is in your mind, for the Lord is with you'" (2Sa. 7:1-3).

Sent Word through Nathan the Prophet

"Then David comforted his wife Bathsheba, and went in to her and lay with her; and she gave birth to a son, and he named him Solomon. Now the

Lord loved him and sent word through Nathan the prophet, and he named him Jedidiah for the Lord's sake" (2Sa. 12:24-25).

The Word of the Lord Came to the Prophet Gad

"Now David's heart troubled him after he had numbered the people. So David said to the Lord, 'I have sinned greatly in what I have done. But now, O Lord, please take away the iniquity of Thy servant, for I have acted very foolishly.' When David arose in the morning, the word of the Lord came to the prophet Gad, David's seer, saying, 'Go and speak to David, 'Thus the Lord says, 'I am offering you three things; choose for yourself one of them, which I may do to you.''' So Gad came to David and told him, and said to him, 'Shall seven years of famine come to you in your land? Or will you flee three months before your foes while they pursue you? Or shall there be three days' pestilence in your land? Now consider and see what answer I shall return to Him who sent me.' Then David said to Gad, 'I am in great distress. Let us now fall into the hand of the Lord for His mercies are great, but do not let me fall into the hand of man'" (2Sa. 24:10-14).

IN THE BOOK OF 1 KINGS

Nathan the Prophet Belonged to David

"Now Adonijah the son of Haggith exalted himself, saying, 'I will be king.' So he prepared for himself chariots and horsemen with fifty men to run before him. And his father had never crossed him at any time by asking, 'Why have you done so?' And he was also a very handsome man; and he was born after Absalom. And he had conferred with Joab the son of Zeruiah and with Abiathar the priest; and following Adonijah they helped him. But Zadok the priest, Benaiah the son of Jehoiada, Nathan the prophet, Shimei, Rei, and the mighty men who belonged to David, were not with Adonijah. And Adonijah sacrificed sheep and oxen and fatlings by the stone of Zoheleth, which is beside En-rogel; and he invited all his brothers, the king's sons, and all the men of Judah, the king's servants. But he did not invite Nathan the prophet, Benaiah, the mighty men, and Solomon his brother" (1Ki. 1:5-10).

While She Was Still Speaking with the King, Nathan the Prophet Came In

"And behold, while she was still speaking with the king, Nathan the prophet came in. And they told the king, saying, 'Here is Nathan the prophet.' And when he came in before the king, he prostrated himself before the king with his face to the ground. Then Nathan said, 'My lord the king, have you said, "Adonijah shall be king after me, and he shall sit on my throne"? For he has gone down today and has sacrificed oxen and fatlings and sheep in abundance, and has invited all the king's sons and the commanders of the army and Abiathar the priest, and behold, they are eating and drinking before him; and they say, "Long live King Adonijah!" But me, even me your servant, and Zadok the priest and Benaiah the son of Jehoiada and your servant Solomon, he has not invited. Has this thing been done by my lord the king, and you have not shown to your servants who should sit on the throne of my lord the king after him?'" (1Ki. 1:22-27).

King David Said Call to Me Nathan the Prophet

"Then King David said, 'Call to me Zadok the priest, Nathan the prophet, and Benaiah the son of Jehoiada.' And they came into the king's presence. And the king said to them, 'Take with you the servants of your lord, and have my son Solomon ride on my own mule, and bring him down to Gihon. And let Zadok the priest and Nathan the prophet anoint him there as king over Israel, and blow the trumpet and say, "Long live King Solomon!" Then you shall come up after him, and he shall come and sit on my throne and be king in my place; for I have appointed him to be ruler over Israel and Judah.' And Benaiah the son of Jehoiada answered the king and said, 'Amen! Thus may the Lord, the God of my lord the king, say. As the Lord has been with my lord the king, so may He be with Solomon, and make his throne greater than the throne of my lord King David!" (1Ki. 1:32-37).

Nathan the Prophet, Benaiah and Mighty Men

"So Zadok the priest, Nathan the prophet, Benaiah the son of Jehoiada, the Cherethites, and the Pelethites went down and had Solomon ride on King David's mule, and brought him to Gihon. Zadok the priest then took the horn of oil from the tent and anointed Solomon. Then they blew the trumpet, and all the people said, 'Long live King Solomon!' And all the people went up after him, and the people were playing on flutes and rejoicing with great joy, so that the earth shook at their noise. Now Adonijah and all the guests who were with him heard it, as they finished eating. When Joab heard the sound of the trumpet, he said, 'Why is the city making such an uproar?' While he was still speaking, behold, Jonathan the son of Abiathar the priest came. Then Adonijah said, 'Come in, for you are a valiant man and bring good news.' But Jonathan answered and said to Adonijah, 'No! Our lord King David has made Solomon king. The king has also sent with him Zadok the priest, Nathan the prophet, Benaiah the son of Jehoiada, the Cherethites, and the Pelethites; and they have made him ride on the king's mule. And Zadok the priest and Nathan the prophet have anointed him king in Gihon, and they have come up from there rejoicing, so that the city is in an uproar. This is the noise which you have heard. Besides, Solomon has even taken his seat on the throne of the kingdom. And moreover, the king's servants came to bless our lord King David, saying, "May your God make the name of Solomon better than your name and his throne greater than your throne!" And the king bowed himself on the bed. The king has also said thus, "Blessed be the Lord, the God of Israel, who has granted one to sit on my throne today while my own eyes see it"'" (1Ki. 1:38-48).

The Prophet Found Him on the Road

"Then Jeroboam the son of Nebat, an Ephraimite of Zeredah, Solomon's servant, whose mother's name was Zeruah, a widow, also rebelled against the king. Now this was the reason why he rebelled against the king: Solomon built the Millo, and closed up the breach of the city of his father David. Now the man Jeroboam was a valiant warrior, and when Solomon saw that the young man was industrious, he appointed him over all the forced labor of the house of Joseph. And it came about at that time, when Jeroboam went out of Jerusalem, that the prophet Ahijah the Shilonite found him on the road. Now Ahijah had clothed himself with a new cloak; and both of them were alone in the field. Then Ahijah took hold of the new cloak which was on him, and tore it into twelve pieces. And he said to Jeroboam, 'Take for yourself ten pieces; for thus says the Lord, the God of Israel, "Behold, I will tear the kingdom out of the hand of Solomon and give you ten tribes (but he will have one tribe, for the sake of My servant David and for the sake of Jerusalem, the city which I have chosen from all the tribes of Israel), because they have forsaken Me, and have worshiped Ashtoreth the goddess of the Sidonians, Chemosh the god of Moab, and Milcom the god of the sons of Ammon; and they have not walked in My ways, doing what is right in My sight and observing My statutes and My ordinances, as his father David did. 'Nevertheless I will not take the whole kingdom out of his hand, but I will make him ruler all the days of his life, for the sake of My servant David whom I chose, who observed My commandments and My statutes; but I will take the kingdom from his son's hand and give it to you, even ten tribes. But to his son I will give one tribe, that My servant David may have a lamp always before Me in Jerusalem, the city where I have chosen for Myself to put My name. And I will take you, and you shall reign over whatever you desire, and you shall be king over Israel. Then it will be, that if you listen to all that I command you and walk in My ways, and do what is right in My sight by observing My statutes and My commandments, as My servant David did, then I will be with you and build you an enduring house as I built for David, and I will give Israel to you. 'Thus I will afflict the descendants of David for this, but not always.'" Solomon sought therefore to put Jeroboam to death; but Jeroboam arose and fled to Egypt to Shishak king of Egypt, and he was in Egypt until the death of Solomon" (1Ki. 11:26-40).

An Old Prophet was Living in Bethel

"Now an old prophet was living in Bethel; and his sons came and told him all the deeds which the man of God had done that day in Bethel; the words which he had spoken to the king, these also they related to their father. Their father said to them, 'Which way did he go?' Now his sons had seen the way which the man of God who came from Judah had gone. Then he said to his sons, 'Saddle the donkey for me.' So they saddled the donkey for him and he rode away on it. So he went after the man of God and found him sitting under an oak; and he said to him, 'Are you the man of God who came from Judah?' And he said, 'I am.' Then he said to him, 'Come home with me and eat bread.' He said, 'I cannot return with you, nor go with you, nor will I eat bread or drink water with you in this place. For a command came to me by the word of the Lord, 'You shall eat no bread, nor drink water there; do not return by going the way which you came.' He said to him, 'I also am a prophet like you, and an angel spoke to me by the word of the Lord, saying, "Bring him back with you to your house, that he may eat bread and drink water."' But he lied to him. So he went back with him, and ate bread in his house and drank water" (1Ki. 13:11-19).

The Word of the Lord Came to the Prophet

"Now it came about, as they were sitting down at the table, that the word of the Lord came to the prophet who had brought him back; and he cried to the man of God who came from Judah, saying, 'Thus says the Lord, "Because you have disobeyed the command of the Lord, and have not observed the commandment which the Lord your God commanded you, but have returned and eaten bread and drunk water in the place of which He said to you, 'Eat no bread and drink no water'; your body shall not come to the grave of your fathers.'"' It came about after he had eaten bread and after he had drunk, that he saddled the donkey for him, for the prophet whom he had brought back. Now when he had gone, a lion met him on the way and killed him, and his body was thrown on the road, with the donkey standing beside it; the lion also was standing beside the body. And behold, men passed by and saw the body thrown on the road, and the lion standing beside the body; so they came and told it in the city where the old prophet lived" (1Ki. 13:20-25).

Chapter Two

The Prophet Laid the Body on the Donkey

"Now when the prophet who brought him back from the way heard it, he said, 'It is the man of God, who disobeyed the command of the Lord; therefore the Lord has given him to the lion, which has torn him and killed him, according to the word of the Lord which He spoke to him.' Then he spoke to his sons, saying, 'Saddle the donkey for me.' And they saddled it. He went and found his body thrown on the road with the donkey and the lion standing beside the body; the lion had not eaten the body nor torn the donkey. So the prophet took up the body of the man of God and laid it on the donkey and brought it back, and he came to the city of the old prophet to mourn and to bury him. He laid his body in his own grave, and they mourned over him, saying, 'Alas, my brother!' After he had buried him, he spoke to his sons, saying, 'When I die, bury me in the grave in which the man of God is buried; lay my bones beside his bones. For the thing shall surely come to pass which he cried by the word of the Lord against the altar in Bethel and against all the houses of the high places which are in the cities of Samaria'" (1Ki. 13:26-32).

Ahijah the Prophet

"At that time Abijah the son of Jeroboam became sick. Jeroboam said to his wife, 'Arise now, and disguise yourself so that they will not know that you are the wife of Jeroboam, and go to Shiloh; behold, Ahijah the prophet is there, who spoke concerning me that I would be king over this people.

Take ten loaves with you, some cakes and a jar of honey, and go to him. He will tell you what will happen to the boy'" (1Ki. 14:1-3).

He Spoke Through His Servant Ahijah the Prophet

"Then Jeroboam's wife arose and departed and came to Tirzah. As she was entering the threshold of the house, the child died. All Israel buried him and mourned for him, according to the word of the Lord which He spoke through His servant Ahijah the prophet" (1Ki. 14:17-18).

The Word of the Lord Through the Prophet Jehu

"Now the rest of the acts of Baasha and what he did and his might, are they not written in the Book of the Chronicles of the Kings of Israel? And Baasha slept with his fathers and was buried in Tirzah, and Elah his son became king in his place. Moreover, the word of the Lord through the prophet Jehu the son of Hanani also came against Baasha and his household, both because of all the evil which he did in the sight of the Lord, provoking Him to anger with the work of his hands, in being like the house of Jeroboam, and because he struck it" (1Ki. 16:5-7).

Which He Spoke Through Jehu the Prophet

"Thus Zimri destroyed all the household of Baasha, according to the word of the Lord, which He spoke against Baasha through Jehu the prophet, for all the sins of Baasha and the sins of Elah his son, which they sinned and which they made Israel sin, provoking the Lord God of Israel to anger with their idols. Now the rest of the acts of Elah and all that he did, are they not written in the Book of the Chronicles of the Kings of Israel" (1Ki. 16:12-14)?

Elijah Said to the People, I Alone Am Left a Prophet

"So Ahab sent a message among all the sons of Israel and brought the prophets together at Mount Carmel. Elijah came near to all the people and said, 'How long will you hesitate between two opinions? If the Lord is God, follow Him; but if Baal, follow him.' But the people did not answer him a word. Then Elijah said to the people, 'I alone am left a prophet of the Lord, but Baal's prophets are 450 men. Now let them give us two oxen; and let them choose one ox for themselves and cut it up, and place it on the wood, but put no fire under it; and I will prepare the other ox and lay it on the wood, and I will not put a fire under it. Then you call on the name of your god, and I will call on the name of the Lord, and the God who answers by fire, He is God.' And all the people said, 'That is a good idea.' So Elijah said to the prophets of Baal, 'Choose one ox for yourselves and prepare it first for you are many, and call on the name of your god, but put no fire under it.' Then they took the ox which was given them and they prepared it and called on the name of Baal from morning until noon saying, 'O Baal, answer us.' But there was no voice and no one answered. And they leaped about the altar which they made. It came about at noon, that Elijah mocked them and said, 'Call out with a loud voice, for he is a god; either he is occupied or gone aside, or is on a journey, or perhaps he is asleep and needs to be awakened.' So they cried with a loud voice and cut themselves according to their custom with swords and lances until the blood gushed out on them. When midday was past, they raved until the time of the offering of the evening sacrifice; but there was no voice, no one answered, and no one paid attention" (1Ki. 18:20-29).

Elijah the Prophet

"Then Elijah said to all the people, 'Come near to me.' So all the people came near to him. And he repaired the altar of the Lord which had been torn down. Elijah took twelve stones according to the number of the tribes of the sons of Jacob, to whom the word of the Lord had come, saying, 'Israel shall be your name.' So with the stones he built an altar in the name of the Lord, and he made a trench around the altar, large enough to hold two measures of seed. Then he arranged the wood and cut the ox in pieces and laid it on the wood. And he said, 'Fill four pitchers with water and pour it on the burnt offering and on the wood.' And he said, 'Do it a second time,' and they did it a second time. And he said, 'Do it a third time,' and they did it a third time. The water flowed around the altar and he also filled the trench with water. At the time of the offering of the evening sacrifice, Elijah the prophet came near and said, 'O Lord, the God of Abraham, Isaac and Israel, today let it be known that You are God in Israel and that I am Your servant and I have done all these things at Your word. Answer me, O Lord, answer me, that this people may know that You, O Lord, are God, and that You have turned their heart back again.' Then the fire of the Lord fell and consumed the burnt offering and the wood and the stones and the dust, and licked up the water that was in the trench. When all the people saw it, they fell on their faces; and they said, 'The Lord, He is God; the Lord, He is God'" (1Ki. 18:30-39).

You Shall Anoint as Prophet in Your Place

"The Lord said to him, 'Go, return on your way to the wilderness of Damascus, and when you have arrived, you shall anoint Hazael king over Aram; and Jehu the son of Nimshi you shall anoint king over Israel; and Elisha the son of Shaphat of Abel-meholah you shall anoint as prophet in your place. It shall come about, the one who escapes from the sword of Hazael, Jehu shall put to death, and the one who escapes from the sword of Jehu, Elisha shall put to death. Yet I will leave 7,000 in Israel, all the knees that have not bowed to Baal and every mouth that has not kissed him'" (1Ki. 19:15-18).

A Prophet Approached Ahab king of Israel

"Now behold, a prophet approached Ahab king of Israel and said, 'Thus says the Lord, "Have you seen all this great multitude? Behold, I will deliver them into your hand today, and you shall know that I am the Lord.'" Ahab said, 'By whom?' So he said, 'Thus says the Lord, "By the young men of the rulers of the provinces."' Then he said, 'Who shall begin the battle?' And he answered, 'You.'

Chapter Two

Then he mustered the young men of the rulers of the provinces, and there were 232; and after them he mustered all the people, even all the sons of Israel, 7,000" (1Ki. 20:13-15).

The Prophet Said Go Strengthen Yourself

"Then the prophet came near to the king of Israel and said to him, 'Go, strengthen yourself and observe and see what you have to do; for at the turn of the year the king of Aram will come up against you'" (1Ki. 20:22).

The Prophet Departed and Waited for the King

"Now a certain man of the sons of the prophets said to another by the word of the Lord, 'Please strike me.' But the man refused to strike him. Then he said to him, 'Because you have not listened to the voice of the Lord, behold, as soon as you have departed from me, a lion will kill you.' And as soon as he had departed from him a lion found him and killed him. Then he found another man and said, 'Please strike me.' And the man struck him, wounding him. So the prophet departed and waited for the king by the way, and disguised himself with a bandage over his eyes. As the king passed by, he cried to the king and said, 'Your servant went out into the midst of the battle; and behold, a man turned aside and brought a man to me and said, 'Guard this man; if for any reason he is missing, then your life shall be for his life, or else you shall pay a talent of silver.' While your servant was busy here and there, he was gone. And the king of Israel said to him, 'So shall your judgment be; you yourself have decided it.' Then he hastily took the bandage away from his eyes, and the king of Israel recognized him that he was of the prophets. He said to him, 'Thus says the Lord, "Because you have let go out of your hand the man whom I had devoted to destruction, therefore your life shall go for his life, and your people for his people.'" So the king of Israel went to his house sullen and vexed, and came to Samaria" (1Ki. 20:35-43).

Is There Not Yet a Prophet of the Lord Here

"Moreover, Jehoshaphat said to the king of Israel, 'Please inquire first for the word of the Lord.' Then the king of Israel gathered the prophets together, about four hundred men, and said to them, 'Shall I go against Ramoth-gilead to battle or shall I refrain?' And they said, 'Go up, for the Lord will give it into the hand of the king.' But Jehoshaphat said, 'Is there not yet a prophet of the Lord here that we may inquire of him?' The king of Israel said to Jehoshaphat, 'There is yet one man by whom we may inquire of the Lord, but I hate him, because he does not prophesy good concerning me, but evil. He is Micaiah son of Imlah.' But Jehoshaphat said, 'Let not the king say so.' Then the king of Israel called an officer and said, 'Bring quickly Micaiah son of Imlah.' Now the king of Israel and Jehoshaphat king of Judah were sitting each on his throne, arrayed in their robes, at the threshing floor at the entrance of the gate of Samaria; and all the prophets were prophesying before them. Then Zedekiah the son of Chenaanah made horns of iron for himself and said,

'Thus says the Lord, "With these you will gore the Arameans until they are consumed."' All the prophets were prophesying thus, saying, 'Go up to Ramoth-gilead and prosper, for the Lord will give it into the hand of the king'" (1Ki. 22:5-12).

IN THE BOOK OF 2 KINGS

No Prophets to Inquire of the Lord by Him

"So the king of Israel went with the king of Judah and the king of Edom; and they made a circuit of seven days' journey, and there was no water for the army or for the cattle that followed them. Then the king of Israel said, 'Alas! For the Lord has called these three kings to give them into the hand of Moab.' But Jehoshaphat said, 'Is there not a prophet of the Lord here, that we may inquire of the Lord by him?' And one of the king of Israel's servants answered and said, 'Elisha the son of Shaphat is here, who used to pour water on the hands of Elijah.' Jehoshaphat said, 'The word of the Lord is with him.' So the king of Israel and Jehoshaphat and the king of Edom went down to him" (2Ki. 3:9-12).

I Wish That My Master Were With the Prophet

"Now Naaman, captain of the army of the king of Aram, was a great man with his master, and highly respected, because by him the Lord had given victory to Aram. The man was also a valiant warrior, but he was a leper. Now the Arameans had gone out in bands and had taken captive a little girl from the land of Israel; and she waited on Naaman's wife. She said to her mistress, 'I wish that my master were with the prophet who is in Samaria! Then he would cure him of his leprosy.' Naaman went in and told his master, saying, 'Thus and thus spoke the girl who is from the land of Israel.' Then the king of Aram said, 'Go now, and I will send a letter to the king of Israel.' He departed and took with him ten talents of silver and six thousand shekels of gold and ten changes of clothes" (2Ki. 5:1-5).

He Shall Know that There Is a Prophet in Israel

"It happened when Elisha the man of God heard that the king of Israel had torn his clothes, that he sent word to the king, saying, 'Why have you torn your clothes? Now let him come to me, and he shall know that there is a prophet in Israel.' So Naaman came with his horses and his chariots and stood at the doorway of the house of Elisha. Elisha sent a messenger to him, saying, 'Go and wash in the Jordan seven times, and your flesh will be restored to you and you will be clean.' But Naaman was furious and went away and said, 'Behold, I thought, 'He will surely come out to me and stand and call on the name of the Lord his God, and wave his hand over the place and cure the leper.' Are not Abanah and Pharpar, the rivers of Damascus, better than all the waters of Israel? Could I not wash in them and be clean?' So he turned and went away in a rage. Then his servants came near and spoke to him and said, 'My father, had the prophet told you to do some great thing, would you not have done it? How much more then, when he says to you, "Wash, and be clean"?' So he went down and dipped himself seven times in the Jordan, according to the word of the man of God; and his flesh was restored like the flesh of a little child and he was clean" (2Ki. 5:8-14).

Elisha, the Prophet Who Is in Israel

"Now the heart of the king of Aram was enraged over this thing; and he called his servants and said to them, 'Will you tell me which of us is for the king of Israel?' One of his servants said, 'No, my lord, O king; but Elisha, the prophet who is in Israel, tells the king of Israel the words that you speak in your bedroom.' So he said, 'Go and see where he is, that I may send and take him.' And it was told him, saying, 'Behold, he is in Dothan.' He sent horses and chariots and a great army there, and they came by night and surrounded the city" (2Ki. 6:11-14).

Elisha the Prophet Told Him Gird up Your Loins

"Now Elisha the prophet called one of the sons of the prophets and said to him, 'Gird up your loins, and take this flask of oil in your hand and go to Ramoth-gilead. When you arrive there, search out Jehu the son of Jehoshaphat the son of Nimshi, and go in and bid him arise from among his brothers, and bring him to an inner room. Then take the flask of oil and pour it on his head and say, "Thus says the Lord, 'I have anointed you king over Israel.'"' Then open the door and flee and do not wait'" (2Ki. 9:1-3).

Chapter Two

The Servant of the Prophet

"So the young man, the servant of the prophet, went to Ramoth-gilead. When he came, behold, the captains of the army were sitting, and he said, 'I have a word for you, O captain.' And Jehu said, 'For which one of us?' And he said, 'For you, O captain.' He arose and went into the house, and he poured the oil on his head and said to him, 'Thus says the Lord, the God of Israel, "I have anointed you king over the people of the Lord, even over Israel. You shall strike the house of Ahab your master, that I may avenge the blood of My servants the prophets, and the blood of all the servants of the Lord, at the hand of Jezebel. For the whole house of Ahab shall perish, and I will cut off from Ahab every male person both bond and free in Israel. I will make the house of Ahab like the house of Jeroboam the son of Nebat, and like the house of Baasha the son of Ahijah. The dogs shall eat Jezebel in the territory of Jezreel, and none shall bury her."' Then he opened the door and fled" (2Ki. 9:4-10).

He Spoke Through His Servant the Prophet

"In the fifteenth year of Amaziah the son of Joash king of Judah, Jeroboam the son of Joash king of Israel became king in Samaria, and reigned forty-one years. He did evil in the sight of the Lord; he did not depart from all the sins of Jeroboam the son of Nebat, which he made Israel sin. He restored the border of Israel from the entrance of Hamath as far as the Sea of the Arabah, according to the word of the Lord, the God of Israel, which He spoke through

Chapter Two

His servant Jonah the son of Amittai, the prophet, who was of Gath-hepher. For the Lord saw the affliction of Israel, which was very bitter; for there was neither bond nor free, nor was there any helper for Israel. The Lord did not say that He would blot out the name of Israel from under heaven, but He saved them by the hand of Jeroboam the son of Joash" (2Ki. 14:23-27).

To Isaiah the Prophet

"And when King Hezekiah heard it, he tore his clothes, covered himself with sackcloth and entered the house of the Lord. Then he sent Eliakim who was over the household with Shebna the scribe and the elders of the priests, covered with sackcloth, to Isaiah the prophet the son of Amoz. They said to him, 'Thus says Hezekiah, "This day is a day of distress, rebuke, and rejection; for children have come to birth and there is no strength to deliver. Perhaps the Lord your God will hear all the words of Rabshakeh, whom his master the king of Assyria has sent to reproach the living God, and will rebuke the words which the Lord your God has heard. Therefore, offer a prayer for the remnant that is left.'" So the servants of King Hezekiah came to Isaiah. Isaiah said to them, 'Thus you shall say to your master, "Thus says the Lord, 'Do not be afraid because of the words that you have heard, with which the servants of the king of Assyria have blasphemed Me. Behold, I will put a spirit in him so that he will hear a rumor and return to his own land. And I will make him fall by the sword in his own land'"'" (2Ki. 19:1-7).

Chapter Two

Isaiah the Prophet Said Set Your House in Order

"In those days Hezekiah became mortally ill. And Isaiah the prophet the son of Amoz came to him and said to him, 'Thus says the Lord, "Set your house in order, for you shall die and not live."' Then he turned his face to the wall and prayed to the Lord, saying, 'Remember now, O Lord, I beseech You, how I have walked before You in truth and with a whole heart and have done what is good in Your sight.' And Hezekiah wept bitterly. Before Isaiah had gone out of the middle court, the word of the Lord came to him, saying, 'Return and say to Hezekiah the leader of My people, "Thus says the Lord, the God of your father David, 'I have heard your prayer, I have seen your tears; behold, I will heal you. On the third day you shall go up to the house of the Lord. I will add fifteen years to your life, and I will deliver you and this city from the hand of the king of Assyria; and I will defend this city for My own sake and for My servant David's sake."' Then Isaiah said, 'Take a cake of figs.' And they took and laid it on the boil, and he recovered" (2Ki. 20:1-7).

Isaiah the Prophet Cried to the Lord

"Now Hezekiah said to Isaiah, 'What will be the sign that the Lord will heal me, and that I shall go up to the house of the Lord the third day?' Isaiah said, 'This shall be the sign to you from the Lord, that the Lord will do the thing that He has spoken: shall the shadow go forward ten steps or go back ten steps?' So Hezekiah answered, 'It is easy for the shadow to decline ten steps; no, but let the shadow turn backward ten steps.' Isaiah the prophet cried to the Lord, and He brought the shadow on the stairway back ten steps by which it had gone down on the stairway of Ahaz" (2Ki. 20:8-11).

Isaiah the Prophet Came to King Hezekiah

"At that time Berodach-baladan a son of Baladan, king of Babylon, sent letters and a present to Hezekiah, for he heard that Hezekiah had been sick. Hezekiah listened to them, and showed them all his treasure house, the silver and the gold and the spices and the precious oil and the house of his armor and all that was found in his treasuries. There was nothing in his house nor in all his dominion that Hezekiah did not show them. Then Isaiah the prophet came to King Hezekiah and said to him, 'What did these men say, and from where have they come to you?' And Hezekiah said, 'They have come from a far country, from Babylon.' He said, 'What have they seen in your house?' So Hezekiah answered, 'They have seen all that is in my house; there is nothing among my treasuries that I have not shown them'" (2Ki. 20:12-15).

The Bones of the Prophet

"Furthermore, the altar that was at Bethel and the high place which Jeroboam the son of Nebat, who made Israel sin, had made, even that altar and the high place he broke down. Then he demolished its stones, ground them to dust, and burned the Asherah. Now when Josiah turned, he saw the graves that were there on the mountain, and he sent and took the bones from the graves and burned them on the altar and defiled it according to the word of the Lord which the man of God proclaimed, who proclaimed these things. Then he said, 'What is this monument that I see?' And the men of the city told him, 'It is the grave of the man of God who came from Judah and proclaimed these things which you have done against the altar of Bethel.' He said, 'Let him alone; let no one disturb his bones.' So they left his bones undisturbed with the bones of the prophet who came from Samaria. Josiah also removed all the houses of the high places which were in the cities of Samaria, which the kings of Israel had made provoking the Lord; and he did to them just as he had done in Bethel. All the priests of the high places who were there he slaughtered on the altars and burned human bones on them; then he returned to Jerusalem" (2Ki. 23:15-20).

IN THE BOOK OF 1 CHRONICLES

David Spoke to Nathan the Prophet

"And it came about, when David dwelt in his house, that David said to Nathan the prophet, 'Behold, I am dwelling in a house of cedar, but the ark of the covenant of the Lord is under curtains.' Then Nathan said to David, 'Do all that is in your heart, for God is with you.' It came about the same night that the word of God came to Nathan, saying, 'Go and tell David My servant, "Thus says the Lord, 'You shall not build a house for Me to dwell in; for I have not dwelt in a house since the day that I brought up Israel to this day, but I have gone from tent to tent and from one dwelling place to another. In all places where I have walked with all Israel, have I spoken a word with any of the judges of Israel, whom I commanded to shepherd My people, saying, "Why have you not built for Me a house of cedar?"' Now, therefore, thus shall you say to My servant David, "Thus says the Lord of hosts, 'I took you from the pasture, from following the sheep, to be leader over My people Israel. I have been with you wherever you have gone, and have cut off all your enemies from before you; and I will make you a name like the name of the great ones who are in the earth. I will appoint a place for My people Israel, and will plant them, so that they may dwell in their own place and not be moved again; and the wicked will not waste them anymore as formerly, even from the day that I commanded judges to be over My people Israel. And I will subdue all your enemies. Moreover, I tell you that the Lord will build a house for you. When your days are fulfilled that you must go to be with your fathers, that I will set up one of your descendants after you, who will be of your sons; and I will establish his kingdom. He shall build for Me a house, and I will establish his throne forever. I will be his father and he shall be My son; and I will not take My lovingkindness away from him, as I took it from him who was before you. But I will settle him in My house and in My kingdom forever, and his throne shall be established forever."'" According to all these words and according to all this vision, so Nathan spoke to David" (1Ch. 17:1-15).

Chapter Two

In the Chronicles of Nathan the Prophet

"Now David the son of Jesse reigned over all Israel. The period which he reigned over Israel was forty years; he reigned in Hebron seven years and in Jerusalem thirty-three years. Then he died in a ripe old age, full of days, riches and honor; and his son Solomon reigned in his place. Now the acts of King David, from first to last, are written in the chronicles of Samuel the seer, in the chronicles of Nathan the prophet and in the chronicles of Gad the seer, with all his reign, his power, and the circumstances which came on him, on Israel, and on all the kingdoms of the lands" (1Ch. 29:26-30).

IN THE BOOK OF 2 CHRONICLES

The Records of Nathan the Prophet

"Now the rest of the acts of Solomon, from first to last, are they not written in the records of Nathan the prophet, and in the prophecy of Ahijah the Shilonite, and in the visions of Iddo the seer concerning Jeroboam the son of Nebat? Solomon reigned forty years in Jerusalem over all Israel. And Solomon slept with his fathers and was buried in the city of his father David; and his son Rehoboam reigned in his place" (2Ch. 9:29-31).

Shemaiah the Prophet

"When the kingdom of Rehoboam was established and strong, he and all Israel with him forsook the law of the Lord. And it came about in

Chapter Two

King Rehoboam's fifth year, because they had been unfaithful to the Lord, that Shishak king of Egypt came up against Jerusalem with 1,200 chariots and 60,000 horsemen. And the people who came with him from Egypt were without number: the Lubim, the Sukkiim and the Ethiopians. He captured the fortified cities of Judah and came as far as Jerusalem. Then Shemaiah the prophet came to Rehoboam and the princes of Judah who had gathered at Jerusalem because of Shishak, and he said to them, 'Thus says the Lord, "You have forsaken Me, so I also have forsaken you to Shishak."' So the princes of Israel and the king humbled themselves and said, 'The Lord is righteous'" (2Ch. 12:1-6).

Shemaiah the Prophet and of Iddo the Seer

"Now the acts of Rehoboam, from first to last, are they not written in the records of Shemaiah the prophet and of Iddo the seer, according to genealogical enrollment? And there were wars between Rehoboam and Jeroboam continually. And Rehoboam slept with his fathers and was buried in the city of David; and his son Abijah became king in his place" (2Ch. 12:15-16).

Written in the Treatise of the Prophet Iddo

"But Abijah became powerful; and took fourteen wives to himself, and became the father of twenty-two sons and sixteen daughters. Now the rest of the acts of Abijah, and his ways and his words are written in the treatise of the prophet Iddo" (2Ch. 13:21-22).

Chapter Two

The Prophet Spoke

"Now when Asa heard these words and the prophecy which Azariah the son of Oded the prophet spoke, he took courage and removed the abominable idols from all the land of Judah and Benjamin and from the cities which he had captured in the hill country of Ephraim. He then restored the altar of the Lord which was in front of the porch of the Lord. He gathered all Judah and Benjamin and those from Ephraim, Manasseh and Simeon who resided with them, for many defected to him from Israel when they saw that the Lord his God was with him. So they assembled at Jerusalem in the third month of the fifteenth year of Asa's reign. They sacrificed to the Lord that day 700 oxen and 7,000 sheep from the spoil they had brought. They entered into the covenant to seek the Lord God of their fathers with all their heart and soul; and whoever would not seek the Lord God of Israel should be put to death, whether small or great, man or woman. Moreover, they made an oath to the Lord with a loud voice, with shouting, with trumpets and with horns. All Judah rejoiced concerning the oath, for they had sworn with their whole heart and had sought Him earnestly, and He let them find Him. So the Lord gave them rest on every side" (2Ch. 15:8-15).

A Prophet That We May Inquire of Him

"Moreover, Jehoshaphat said to the king of Israel, 'Please inquire first for the word of the Lord.' Then the king of Israel assembled the prophets, four hundred men, and said to them, 'Shall we go against Ramoth-gilead to battle, or shall I refrain?' And they said, 'Go up, for God will give it into the hand of the king.' But Jehoshaphat said, 'Is there not yet a prophet of the Lord here that we may inquire of him?' The king of Israel said to Jehoshaphat, 'There is yet one man by whom we may inquire of the Lord, but I hate him, for he never prophesies good concerning me but always evil. He is Micaiah, son of Imla.' But Jehoshaphat said, 'Let not the king say so.' Then the king of Israel called an officer and said, 'Bring quickly Micaiah, Imla's son.' Now the king of Israel and Jehoshaphat the king of Judah were sitting each on his throne, arrayed in their robes, and they were sitting at the threshing floor at the entrance of the gate of Samaria; and all the prophets were prophesying before them. Zedekiah the son of Chenaanah made horns of iron for himself and said, 'Thus says the Lord, "With these you shall gore the Arameans until they are consumed."' All the prophets were prophesying thus, saying, 'Go up to Ramoth-gilead and succeed, for the Lord will give it into the hand of the king'" (2Ch. 18:4-11).

A Letter Came to Him from Elijah the Prophet

"Then a letter came to him from Elijah the prophet saying, 'Thus says the Lord God of your father David, "Because you have not walked in the ways of Jehoshaphat your father and the ways of Asa king of Judah, but have walked in the way of the kings of Israel, and have caused Judah and the inhabitants of Jerusalem to play the harlot as the house of Ahab played the harlot, and you have also killed your brothers, your own family, who were better than you, behold, the Lord is going to strike your people, your sons, your wives and all your possessions with a great calamity; and you will suffer severe sickness, a disease of your bowels, until your bowels come out because of the sickness, day by day'"" (2Ch. 21:12-15).

He Sent Him a Prophet

"Now after Amaziah came from slaughtering the Edomites, he brought the gods of the sons of Seir, set them up as his gods, bowed down before them and burned incense to them. Then the anger of the Lord burned against Amaziah, and He sent him a prophet who said to him, 'Why have you sought the gods of the people who have not delivered their own people from your hand?' As he was talking with him, the king said to him, 'Have we appointed you a royal counselor? Stop! Why should you be struck down?' Then the prophet stopped and said, 'I know that God has planned to destroy you, because you have done this and have not listened to my counsel'" (2Ch. 25:14-16).

The Prophet Isaiah

"Now the rest of the acts of Uzziah, first to last, the prophet Isaiah, the son of Amoz, has written. So Uzziah slept with his fathers, and they buried him with his fathers in the field of the grave which belonged to the kings, for they said, 'He is a leper.' And Jotham his son became king in his place" (2Ch. 26:22-23).

Chapter Two

A Prophet of the Lord Was There

"The sons of Israel carried away captive of their brethren 200,000 women, sons and daughters; and they took also a great deal of spoil from them, and brought the spoil to Samaria. But a prophet of the Lord was there, whose name was Oded; and he went out to meet the army which came to Samaria and said to them, 'Behold, because the Lord, the God of your fathers, was angry with Judah, He has delivered them into your hand, and you have slain them in a rage which has even reached heaven. Now you are proposing to subjugate for yourselves the people of Judah and Jerusalem for male and female slaves. Surely, do you not have transgressions of your own against the Lord your God? Now therefore, listen to me and return the captives whom you captured from your brothers, for the burning anger of the Lord is against you.' Then some of the heads of the sons of Ephraim — Azariah the son of Johanan, Berechiah the son of Meshillemoth, Jehizkiah the son of Shallum, and Amasa the son of Hadlai — arose against those who were coming from the battle, and said to them, 'You must not bring the captives in here, for you are proposing to bring upon us guilt against the Lord adding to our sins and our guilt; for our guilt is great so that His burning anger is against Israel.' So the armed men left the captives and the spoil before the officers and all the assembly. Then the men who were designated by name arose, took the captives, and they clothed all their naked ones from the spoil; and they gave them clothes and sandals, fed them and gave them drink, anointed them with oil, led all their feeble ones on donkeys, and brought them to Jericho, the city of palm trees, to their brothers; then they returned to Samaria" (2Ch. 28:8-15).

Gad the King's Seer, and Nathan the Prophet

"He then stationed the Levites in the house of the Lord with cymbals, with harps and with lyres, according to the command of David and of Gad the king's seer, and of Nathan the prophet; for the command was from the Lord through His prophets. The Levites stood with the musical instruments of David, and the priests with the trumpets. Then Hezekiah gave the order to offer the burnt offering on the altar. When the burnt offering began, the song to the Lord also began with the trumpets, accompanied by the instruments of David, king of Israel. While the whole assembly worshiped, the singers also sang and the trumpets sounded; all this continued until the burnt offering was finished" (2Ch. 29:25-28).

King Hezekiah and Isaiah the Prophet Prayed

"But King Hezekiah and Isaiah the prophet, the son of Amoz, prayed about this and cried out to heaven. And the Lord sent an angel who destroyed every mighty warrior, commander and officer in the camp of the king of Assyria. So he returned in shame to his own land. And when he had entered the temple of his god, some of his own children killed him there with the sword. So the Lord saved Hezekiah and the inhabitants of Jerusalem from the hand of Sennacherib the king of Assyria and from the hand of all others, and guided them on every side. And many were bringing gifts to the Lord at Jerusalem and choice presents to Hezekiah king of Judah, so that he was exalted in the sight of all nations thereafter" (2Ch. 32:20-23).

Written in the Vision of Isaiah the Prophet

"Now the rest of the acts of Hezekiah and his deeds of devotion, behold, they are written in the vision of Isaiah the prophet, the son of Amoz, in the Book of the Kings of Judah and Israel. So Hezekiah slept with his fathers, and they buried him in the upper section of the tombs of the sons of David; and all Judah and the inhabitants of Jerusalem honored him at his death. And his son Manasseh became king in his place" (2Ch. 32:32-33).

Since the Days of Samuel the Prophet

"So all the service of the Lord was prepared on that day to celebrate the Passover, and to offer burnt offerings on the altar of the Lord according to the command of King Josiah. Thus the sons of Israel who were present celebrated the Passover at that time, and the Feast of Unleavened Bread seven days. There had not been celebrated a Passover like it in Israel since the days of Samuel the prophet; nor had any of the kings of Israel celebrated such a Passover as Josiah did with the priests, the Levites, all Judah and Israel who were present, and the inhabitants of Jerusalem. In the eighteenth year of Josiah's reign this Passover was celebrated" (2Ch. 35:16-19).

Chapter Two

Jeremiah the Prophet Who Spoke for the Lord

"Zedekiah was twenty-one years old when he became king, and he reigned eleven years in Jerusalem. He did evil in the sight of the Lord his God; he did not humble himself before Jeremiah the prophet who spoke for the Lord. He also rebelled against King Nebuchadnezzar who had made him swear allegiance by God. But he stiffened his neck and hardened his heart against turning to the Lord God of Israel. Furthermore, all the officials of the priests and the people were very unfaithful following all the abominations of the nations; and they defiled the house of the Lord which He had sanctified in Jerusalem" (2Ch. 36:11-14).

IN THE BOOK OF EZRA

The Prophets Prophesied to the Jews

"When the prophets, Haggai the prophet and Zechariah the son of Iddo, prophesied to the Jews who were in Judah and Jerusalem in the name of the God of Israel, who was over them, then Zerubbabel the son of Shealtiel and Jeshua the son of Jozadak arose and began to rebuild the house of God which is in Jerusalem; and the prophets of God were with them supporting them" (Ezr. 5:1-2).

Through the Prophesying of Haggai the Prophet and Zechariah

"Then Tattenai, the governor of the province beyond the River, Shethar-bozenai and their colleagues carried out the decree with all diligence, just as King Darius had sent. And the elders of the Jews were successful in building through the prophesying of Haggai the prophet and Zechariah the son of Iddo. And they finished building according to the command of the God of Israel and the decree of Cyrus, Darius, and Artaxerxes king of Persia. This temple was completed on the third day of the month Adar; it was the sixth year of the reign of King Darius" (Ezr. 6:13-15).

IN THE BOOK OF PSALMS

There Is No Longer Any Prophet

"O God, why have You rejected us forever? Why does Your anger smoke against the sheep of Your pasture? Remember Your congregation, which You have purchased of old, Which You have redeemed to be the tribe of Your inheritance; And this Mount Zion, where You have dwelt. Turn Your footsteps toward the perpetual ruins; The enemy has damaged everything within the sanctuary. Your adversaries have roared in the midst of Your meeting place; They have set up their own standards for signs. It seems as if one had lifted up His axe in a forest of trees. And now all its carved work They smash with hatchet and hammers. They have burned Your sanctuary to the ground; They have defiled the dwelling place of Your name. They said in their heart, 'Let us completely subdue them.' They have burned all the meeting places of God in the land. We do not see our signs; There is no longer any prophet, Nor is there any among us who knows how long. How long, O God, will the adversary revile, And the enemy spurn Your name forever? Why do You withdraw Your hand, even Your right hand? From within Your bosom, destroy them" (Ps. 74:1-11)!

IN THE BOOK OF ISAIAH

The Judge and the Prophet

"For behold, the Lord God of hosts is going to remove from Jerusalem and Judah Both supply and support, the whole supply of bread And the whole supply of water; The mighty man and the warrior, The judge and the prophet, The diviner and the elder, The captain of fifty and the honorable man, The counselor and the expert artisan, And the skillful enchanter. And I will make mere lads their princes, And capricious children will rule over them, And the people will be oppressed, Each one by another, and each one by his neighbor; The youth will storm against the elder And the inferior against the honorable. When a man lays hold of his brother in his father's house, saying, 'You have a cloak, you shall be our ruler, And these ruins will be under your charge,' He will protest on that day, saying, 'I will not be your healer, For in my house there is neither bread nor cloak; You should not appoint me ruler of the people.' For Jerusalem has stumbled and Judah has fallen, Because their speech and their actions are against the Lord, To rebel against His glorious presence. The expression of their faces bears witness against them, And they display their sin like Sodom; They do not even conceal it. Woe to them!

For they have brought evil on themselves. Say to the righteous that it will go well with them, For they will eat the fruit of their actions. Woe to the wicked! It will go badly with him, For what he deserves will be done to him. O My people! Their oppressors are children, And women rule over them. O My people! Those who guide you lead you astray And confuse the direction of your paths" (Is. 3:1-12).

The Prophet Who Teaches Falsehood

"Yet the people do not turn back to Him who struck them, Nor do they seek the Lord of hosts. So the Lord cuts off head and tail from Israel, Both palm branch and bulrush in a single day. The head is the elder and honorable man, And the prophet who teaches falsehood is the tail. For those who guide this people are leading them astray; And those who are guided by them are brought to confusion. Therefore the Lord does not take pleasure in their young men, Nor does He have pity on their orphans or their widows; For every one of them is godless and an evildoer, And every mouth is speaking foolishness. In spite of all this, His anger does not turn away And His hand is still stretched out" (Is. 9:13-17).

The Priest and the Prophet Reel with Strong Drink

"Woe to the proud crown of the drunkards of Ephraim, And to the fading flower of its glorious beauty, Which is at the head of the fertile valley Of those who are overcome with wine! Behold, the Lord has a strong and mighty agent;As a storm of hail, a tempest of destruction, Like a storm of mighty overflowing waters, He has cast it down to the earth with His hand. The proud crown of the drunkards of Ephraim is trodden under foot. And the fading flower of its glorious beauty, Which is at the head of the fertile valley, Will be like the first-ripe fig prior to summer, Which one sees, And as soon as it is in his hand, He swallows it. In that day the Lord of hosts will become a beautiful crown And a glorious diadem to the remnant of His people; A spirit of justice for him who sits in judgment, A strength to those who repel the onslaught at the gate. And these also reel with wine and stagger from strong drink: The priest and the prophet reel with strong drink, They are confused by wine, they stagger from strong drink; They reel while having visions, They totter when rendering judgment. For all the tables are full of filthy vomit, without a single clean place" (Is. 28:1-8).

Isaiah the Prophet

"And when King Hezekiah heard it, he tore his clothes, covered himself with sackcloth and entered the house of the Lord. Then he sent Eliakim who was over the household with Shebna the scribe and the elders of the priests, covered with sackcloth, to Isaiah the prophet, the son of Amoz. They said to him, 'Thus says Hezekiah, "This day is a day of distress, rebuke and rejection; for children have come to birth, and there is no strength to deliver. Perhaps the Lord your God will hear the words of Rabshakeh, whom his master the king of Assyria has sent to reproach the living God, and will rebuke the words which the Lord your God has heard. Therefore, offer a prayer for the remnant that is left"'" (Is. 37:1-4).

Isaiah the Prophet Told Hezekiah Set Your House in Order

"In those days Hezekiah became mortally ill. And Isaiah the prophet the son of Amoz came to him and said to him, 'Thus says the Lord, "Set your house in order, for you shall die and not live.'" Then Hezekiah turned his face to the wall and prayed to the Lord, and said, 'Remember now, O Lord, I beseech You, how I have walked before You in truth and with a whole heart, and have done what is good in Your sight.' And Hezekiah wept bitterly'" (Is. 38:1-3).

Isaiah the Prophet Came to King Hezekiah

"At that time Merodach-baladan son of Baladan, king of Babylon, sent letters and a present to Hezekiah, for he heard that he had been sick and had recovered. Hezekiah was pleased, and showed them all his treasure house, the silver and the gold and the spices and the precious oil and his whole armory and all that was found in his treasuries. There was nothing in his house nor in all his dominion that Hezekiah did not show them. Then Isaiah the prophet came to King Hezekiah and said to him, 'What did these men say, and from where have they come to you?' And Hezekiah said, 'They have come to me from a far country, from Babylon.' He said, 'What have they seen in your house?' So

Hezekiah answered, 'They have seen all that is in my house; there is nothing among my treasuries that I have not shown them'" (Is. 39:1-4).

IN THE BOOK OF JEREMIAH

I Have Appointed You a Prophet to the Nations

"Now the word of the Lord came to me saying, 'Before I formed you in the womb I knew you, And before you were born I consecrated you; I have appointed you a prophet to the natiors.' Then I said, 'Alas, Lord God! Behold, I do not know how to speak, Because I am a youth.' But the Lord said to me, 'Do not say, "I am a youth," Because everywhere I send you, you shall go, And all that I command you, you shall speak. Do not be afraid of them, For I am with you to deliver you,' declares the Lord. Then the Lord stretched out His hand and touched my mouth, and the Lord said to me, 'Behold, I have put My words in your mouth. See, I have appointed you this day over the nations and over the kingdoms, To pluck up and to break down, To destroy and to overthrow, To build and to plant'" (Jer. 1:4-10).

From the Prophet Even to the Priest

"Thus says the Lord of hosts, 'They will thoroughly glean as the vine the remnant of Israel; Pass your hand again like a grape gatherer Over the branches.' To whom shall I speak and give warning That they may hear? Behold, their ears are closed And they cannot listen. Behold, the word of the Lord has become a reproach to them; They have no delight in it. But I am full of the wrath of the Lord; I am weary with holding it in. 'Pour it out on the children in the street And on the gathering of young men together; For both husband and wife shall be taken, The aged and the very old. Their houses shall be turned over to others, Their fields and their wives together; For I will stretch out My hand Against the inhabitants of the land,' declares the Lord. 'For from the least of them even to the greatest of them, Everyone is greedy for gain, And from the prophet even to the priest Everyone deals falsely. They have healed the brokenness of My people superficially, Saying, "Peace, peace," But there is no peace. Were they ashamed because of the abomination they have done? They were not even ashamed at all; They did not even know how to blush. Therefore they shall fall among those who fall; At the time that I punish them, They shall be cast down,' says the Lord" (Jer. 6:9-15).

The Prophet, the Priest and Everyone Practices Deceit

"'How can you say, "We are wise, And the law of the Lord is with us"? But behold, the lying pen of the scribes Has made it into a lie. The wise men are put to shame, They are dismayed and caught; Behold, they have rejected the word of the Lord, And what kind of wisdom do they have? Therefore I will give their wives to others, Their fields to new owners; Because from the least even to the greatest Everyone is greedy for gain; From the prophet even to the priest Everyone practices deceit.

They heal the brokenness of the daughter of My people superficially, Saying, "Peace, peace," But there is no peace. Were they ashamed because of the abomination they had done? They certainly were not ashamed, And they did not know how to blush; Therefore they shall fall among those who fall; At the time of their punishment they shall be brought down,' Says the Lord" (Jer. 8:8-12).

Both Prophet and Priest Have Gone Roving About

"But, 'Ah, Lord God!' I said, 'Look, the prophets are telling them, "You will not see the sword nor will you have famine, but I will give you lasting peace in this place.'" Then the Lord said to me, 'The prophets are prophesying falsehood in My name. I have neither sent them nor commanded them nor spoken to them; they are prophesying to you a false vision, divination, futility and the deception of their own minds. Therefore thus says the Lord concerning the prophets who are prophesying in My name, although it was not I who sent them—yet they keep saying, "There will be no sword or famine in this land"—by sword and famine those prophets shall meet their end! The people also to whom they are prophesying will be thrown out into the streets of Jerusalem because of the famine and the sword; and there will be no one to bury them—neither them, nor their wives, nor their sons, nor their daughters—for I will pour out their own wickedness on them. You will say this word to them, "Let my eyes flow down with tears night and day, And let them not cease; For the virgin daughter of my people has been crushed with a mighty blow,

With a sorely infected wound. If I go out to the country, Behold, those slain with the sword! Or if I enter the city, Behold, diseases of famine! For both prophet and priest Have gone roving about in the land that they do not know"'" (Jer. 14:13-18).

Nor the Divine Word to the Prophet

"Then they said, 'Come and let us devise plans against Jeremiah. Surely the law is not going to be lost to the priest, nor counsel to the sage, nor the divine word to the prophet! Come on and let us strike at him with our tongue, and let us give no heed to any of his words'" (Jer. 18:18).

Pashhur had Jeremiah the Prophet Beaten

"When Pashhur the priest, the son of Immer, who was chief officer in the house of the Lord, heard Jeremiah prophesying these things, Pashhur had Jeremiah the prophet beaten and put him in the stocks that were at the upper Benjamin Gate, which was by the house of the Lord. On the next day, when Pashhur released Jeremiah from the stocks, Jeremiah said to him, 'Pashhur is not the name the Lord has called you, but rather Magor-missabib. For thus says the Lord, "Behold, I am going to make you a terror to yourself and to all your friends; and while your eyes look on, they will fall by the sword of their enemies. So I will give over all Judah to the hand of the king of Babylon, and he will carry them away as exiles to Babylon and will slay them with the sword. I will also give over all the wealth of this city, all its produce and all its costly things; even all the treasures of the kings of Judah I will give over to the hand of their enemies, and they will plunder them, take them away and bring them to Babylon. And you, Pashhur, and all who live in your house will go into captivity; and you will enter Babylon, and there you will die and there you will be buried, you and all your friends to whom you have falsely prophesied"'" (Jer. 20:1-6).

Both Prophet and Priest Are Polluted

"'As for the prophets: My heart is broken within me, All my bones tremble; I have become like a drunken man, Even like a man overcome with wine, Because of the Lord And because of His holy words. For the land is full of adulterers; For the land mourns because of the curse. The pastures of the wilderness have dried up. Their course also is evil And their might is not right. For both prophet and priest are polluted; Even in My house I have found their wickedness,' declares the Lord. 'Therefore their way will be like slippery paths to them, They will be driven away into the gloom and fall down in it; For I will bring calamity upon them, The year of their punishment,' declares the Lord" (Jer. 23:9-12).

The Prophet May Relate His Dream

"'I have heard what the prophets have said who prophesy falsely in My name, saying, 'I had a dream, I had a dream!" How long? Is there anything in the hearts of the prophets who prophesy falsehood, even these prophets of the deception of their own heart, who intend to make My people forget My name by their dreams which they relate to one another, just as their fathers forgot My name because of Baal? The prophet who has a dream may relate his dream, but let him who has My word speak My word in truth. What does straw have in common with grain?' declares the Lord. 'Is not My word like fire?' declares the Lord, 'and like a hammer which shatters a rock? Therefore behold, I am against the prophets,' declares the Lord, 'who steal My words from each other. Behold, I am against the prophets,' declares the Lord, 'who use their tongues and declare, "The Lord declares." Behold, I am against those who have prophesied false dreams,' declares the Lord, 'and related them and led My people astray by their falsehoods and reckless boasting; yet I did not send them or command them, nor do they furnish this people the slightest benefit,' declares the Lord" (Jer. 23:25-32).

This People or the Prophet or a Priest

"Now when this people or the prophet or a priest asks you saying, 'What is the oracle of the Lord?' then you shall say to them, 'What oracle?' The Lord declares, 'I will abandon you.' Then as for the prophet or the priest or the people who say, 'The oracle of the Lord,' I will bring punishment upon that man and his household. Thus will each of you say to his neighbor and to his brother, 'What has the Lord answered?' or, 'What has the Lord spoken?' For you will no longer remember the oracle of the Lord, because every man's own word will become the oracle, and you have perverted the words of the living God, the Lord of hosts, our God. Thus you will say to that prophet, 'What has the Lord answered you?' and, 'What has the Lord spoken?' For if you say, 'The oracle of the Lord!' surely thus says the Lord, 'Because you said this word, "The oracle of the Lord!" I have also sent to you, saying, "You shall not say, 'The oracle of the Lord!'"' Therefore behold, I will surely forget you and cast you away from My presence, along with the city which I gave you and your fathers. I will put an everlasting reproach on you and an everlasting humiliation which will not be forgotten" (Jer. 23:33-40).

Jeremiah the Prophet Spoke to All the People

"The word that came to Jeremiah concerning all the people of Judah, in the fourth year of Jehoiakim the son of Josiah, king of Judah (that was the first year of Nebuchadnezzar king of Babylon), which Jeremiah the prophet spoke to all the people of Judah and to all the inhabitants of Jerusalem, saying, From the thirteenth year of Josiah the son of Amon, king of Judah, even to this day, these twenty-three years the word of the Lord has come to me, and I have spoken to you again and again, but you have not listened. And the Lord has sent to you all His servants the prophets again and again, but you have not listened nor inclined your ear to hear, saying, 'Turn now everyone from his evil way and from the evil of your deeds, and dwell on the land which the Lord has given to you and your forefathers forever and ever; and do not go after other gods to serve them and to worship them, and do not provoke Me to anger with the work of your hands, and I will do you no harm. Yet you have not listened to Me,' declares the Lord, 'in order that you might provoke Me to anger with the work of your hands to your own harm'" (Jer. 25:1-7).

Hananiah the Son of Azzur, the Prophet

"Now in the same year, in the beginning of the reign of Zedekiah king of Judah, in the fourth year, in the fifth month, Hananiah the son of Azzur, the prophet, who was from Gibeon, spoke to me in the house of the Lord in the presence of the priests and all the people, saying, 'Thus says the Lord of hosts, the God of Israel, "I have broken the yoke of the king of Babylon. Within two years I am going to bring back to this place all the vessels of the Lord's house, which Nebuchadnezzar king of Babylon took away from this place and carried to Babylon. I am also going to bring back to this place Jeconiah the son of Jehoiakim, king of Judah, and all the exiles of Judah who went to Babylon,' declares the Lord, "for I will break the yoke of the king of Babylon""' (Jer. 28:1-4).

The Prophet Jeremiah Spoke to the Prophet Hananiah

"Then the prophet Jeremiah spoke to the prophet Hananiah in the presence of the priests and in the presence of all the people who were standing in the house of the Lord, and the prophet Jeremiah said, 'Amen! May the Lord do so; may the Lord confirm your words which you have prophesied to bring back the vessels of the Lord's house and all the exiles, from Babylon to this place. Yet hear now this word which I am about to speak in your hearing and in the hearing of all the people! The prophets who were before me and before you from ancient times prophesied against many lands and against great kingdoms, of war and of calamity and of pestilence. The prophet who prophesies of peace, when the word of the prophet comes to pass, then that prophet will be known as one whom the Lord has truly sent"' (Jer. 28:5-9).

Then Hananiah the Prophet Took the Yoke from the Neck of Jeremiah the Prophet and Broke It

"Then Hananiah the prophet took the yoke from the neck of Jeremiah the prophet and broke it. Hananiah spoke in the presence of all the people, saying, 'Thus says the Lord, "Even so will I break within two full years the yoke of Nebuchadnezzar king of Babylon from the neck of all the nations."' Then the prophet Jeremiah went his way. The word of the Lord came to Jeremiah after Hananiah the prophet had broken the yoke from off the neck of the prophet Jeremiah, saying, 'Go and speak to Hananiah, saying, "Thus says the Lord, 'You have broken the yokes of wood, but you have made instead of them yokes of iron.' 'For thus says the Lord of hosts, the God of Israel, 'I have put a yoke of iron on the neck of all these nations, that they may serve Nebuchadnezzar king of Babylon; and they will serve him. And I have also given him the beasts of the field.'"' Then Jeremiah the prophet said to Hananiah the prophet, 'Listen now, Hananiah, the Lord has not sent you, and you have made this people trust in a lie. Therefore thus says the Lord, "Behold, I am about to remove you from the face of the earth. This year you are going to die, because you have counseled rebellion against the Lord.'" So Hananiah the prophet died in the same year in the seventh month" (Jer. 28:10-17).

Jeremiah the Prophet Sent a Letter

"Now these are the words of the letter which Jeremiah the prophet sent from Jerusalem to the rest of the elders of the exile, the priests, the prophets and all the people whom Nebuchadnezzar had taken into exile from Jerusalem to Babylon. (This was after King Jeconiah and the queen mother, the court officials, the princes of Judah and Jerusalem, the craftsmen and the smiths had departed from Jerusalem.) The letter was sent by the hand of Elasah the son of Shaphan, and Gemariah the son of Hilkiah, whom Zedekiah king of Judah sent to Babylon to Nebuchadnezzar king of Babylon, saying, 'Thus says the Lord of hosts, the God of Israel, to all the exiles whom I have sent into exile from Jerusalem to Babylon, "Build houses and live in them; and plant gardens and eat their produce. Take wives and become the fathers of sons and daughters, and take wives for your sons and give your daughters to husbands, that they may bear sons and daughters; and multiply there and do not decrease. Seek the welfare of the city where I have sent you into exile, and pray to the Lord on its behalf; for in its welfare you will have welfare." For thus says the Lord of hosts, the God of Israel, "Do not let your prophets who are in your midst and your diviners deceive you, and do not listen to the dreams which they dream. For they prophesy falsely to you in My name; I have not sent them," declares the Lord'" (Jer. 29:1-9).

Zephaniah Read the Letter to Jeremiah the Prophet.

"Zephaniah the priest read this letter to Jeremiah the prophet. Then came the word of the Lord to Jeremiah, saying, 'Send to all the exiles, saying, "Thus says the Lord concerning Shemaiah the Nehelamite, 'Because Shemaiah has prophesied to you, although I did not send him, and he has made you trust in a lie,' therefore thus says the Lord, 'Behold, I am about to punish Shemaiah the Nehelamite and his descendants; he will not have anyone living among this people, and he will not see the good that I am about to do to My people,' declares the Lord, 'because he has preached rebellion against the Lord'""" (Jer. 29:29-32).

Jeremiah the Prophet Was Shut up in the Court of the Guard

"The word that came to Jeremiah from the Lord in the tenth year of Zedekiah king of Judah, which was the eighteenth year of Nebuchadnezzar. Now at that time the army of the king of Babylon was besieging Jerusalem, and Jeremiah the prophet was shut up in the court of the guard, which was in the house of the king of Judah, because Zedekiah king of Judah had shut him up, saying, 'Why do you prophesy, saying, "Thus says the Lord, 'Behold, I am about to give this city into the hand of the king of

Babylon, and he will take it; and Zedekiah king of Judah will not escape out of the hand of the Chaldeans, but he will surely be given into the hand of the king of Babylon, and he will speak with him face to face and see him eye to eye; and he will take Zedekiah to Babylon, and he will be there until I visit him,' declares the Lord. 'If you fight against the Chaldeans, you will not succeed""''" (Jer. 32:1-5)?

Jeremiah the Prophet Spoke to Zedekiah

"Then Jeremiah the prophet spoke all these words to Zedekiah king of Judah in Jerusalem when the army of the king of Babylon was fighting against Jerusalem and against all the remaining cities of Judah, that is, Lachish and Azekah, for they alone remained as fortified cities among the cities of Judah. The word which came to Jeremiah from the Lord after King Zedekiah had made a covenant with all the people who were in Jerusalem to proclaim release to them: that each man should set free his male servant and each man his female servant, a Hebrew man or a Hebrew woman; so that no one should keep them, a Jew his brother, in bondage. And all the officials and all the people obeyed who had entered into the covenant that each man should set free his male servant and each man his female servant, so that no one should keep them any longer in bondage; they obeyed, and set them free. But afterward they turned around and took back the male servants and the female servants whom they had set free, and brought them into subjection for male servants and for female servants" (Jer. 34:6-11).

Chapter Two

The Lord Hid Jeremiah the Prophet

"So they went to the king in the court, but they had deposited the scroll in the chamber of Elishama the scribe, and they reported all the words to the king. Then the king sent Jehudi to get the scroll, and he took it out of the chamber of Elishama the scribe. And Jehudi read it to the king as well as to all the officials who stood beside the king. Now the king was sitting in the winter house in the ninth month, with a fire burning in the brazier before him. When Jehudi had read three or four columns, the king cut it with a scribe's knife and threw it into the fire that was in the brazier, until all the scroll was consumed in the fire that was in the brazier. Yet the king and all his servants who heard all these words were not afraid, nor did they rend their garments. Even though Elnathan and Delaiah and Gemariah pleaded with the king not to burn the scroll, he would not listen to them. And the king commanded Jerahmeel the king's son, Seraiah the son of Azriel, and Shelemiah the son of Abdeel to seize Baruch the scribe and Jeremiah the prophet, but the Lord hid them" (Jer. 36:20-26).

They Did Not Listen to the Words of the Lord Which He Spoke Through Jeremiah the Prophet

"Now Zedekiah the son of Josiah whom Nebuchadnezzar king of Babylon had made king in the land of Judah, reigned as king in place of Coniah the son of Jehoiakim. But neither he nor his servants nor the people of the land listened to the words of the Lord which He spoke through Jeremiah the prophet. Yet King Zedekiah sent Jehucal the son of Shelemiah, and Zephaniah the son of Maaseiah, the priest, to Jeremiah the prophet, saying, 'Please pray to the Lord our God on our behalf.' Now Jeremiah was still coming in and going out among the people, for they had not yet put him in the prison. Meanwhile, Pharaoh's army had set out from Egypt; and when the Chaldeans who had been besieging Jerusalem heard the report about them, they lifted the siege from Jerusalem" (Jer. 37:1-5).

The Word of the Lord Came to Jeremiah

"Then the word of the Lord came to Jeremiah the prophet, saying, 'Thus says the Lord God of Israel, "Thus you are to say to the king of Judah, who sent you to Me to inquire of Me: 'Behold, Pharaoh's army which has come out for your assistance is going to return to its own land of Egypt. The Chaldeans will also return and fight against this city, and they will capture it and burn it with fire.'" Thus says the Lord, "Do not deceive yourselves, saying, 'The Chaldeans will surely go away from us,' for they will not go. For even if you had defeated the entire army of Chaldeans who were fighting against you, and there were only wounded men left among them, each man in his tent, they would rise up and burn this city with fire'""" (Jer. 37:6-10).

He Arrested Jeremiah the Prophet

"Now it happened when the army of the Chaldeans had lifted the siege from Jerusalem because of Pharaoh's army, that Jeremiah went out from Jerusalem to go to the land of Benjamin in order to take possession of some property there among the people. While he was at the Gate of Benjamin, a captain of the guard whose name was Irijah, the son of Shelemiah the son of Hananiah was there; and he arrested Jeremiah the prophet, saying, 'You are going over to the Chaldeans!' But Jeremiah said, 'A lie! I am not going over to the Chaldeans'; yet he would not listen to him. So Irijah arrested Jeremiah and brought him to the officials. Then the officials were angry at Jeremiah and beat him, and they put him in jail in the house of Jonathan the scribe, which they had made into the prison. For Jeremiah had come into the dungeon, that is, the vaulted cell; and Jeremiah stayed there many days" (Jer. 37:11-16).

They Acted Wickedly to Jeremiah the Prophet

"Now Shephatiah the son of Mattan, and Gedaliah the son of Pashhur, and Jucal the son of Shelemiah, and Pashhur the son of Malchijah heard the words that Jeremiah was speaking to all the people, saying, 'Thus says the Lord, "He who stays in this city will die by the sword and by famine and by pestilence, but he who goes out to the Chaldeans will live and have his own life as booty and stay alive." Thus says the Lord, "This city will certainly be given into the hand of the army of the king of Babylon and he will capture it."' Then the officials said to the king, 'Now let this man be put to death, inasmuch as he is discouraging the men of war who are left in this city and all the people, by speaking such words to them; for this man is not seeking the well-being of this people but rather their harm.' So King Zedekiah said, 'Behold, he is in your hands; for the king can do nothing against you.' Then they took Jeremiah and cast him into the cistern of Malchijah the king's son, which was in the court of the guardhouse; and they let Jeremiah down with ropes. Now in the cistern there was no water but only mud, and Jeremiah sank into the mud. But Ebed-melech the Ethiopian, a eunuch, while he was in the king's palace, heard that they had put Jeremiah into the cistern. Now the king was sitting in the Gate of Benjamin; and Ebed-melech went out from the king's palace and spoke to the king, saying, 'My lord the king, these men have acted wickedly in all that they have done to Jeremiah the prophet whom they have cast into the cistern; and he will die right where he is because of the famine, for there is no more bread in the city.' Then the king commanded Ebed-melech the Ethiopian, saying, 'Take thirty men from here under your authority and bring up Jeremiah the prophet from the cistern before he dies.' So Ebed-melech took the men under his authority and went into the king's palace to a place beneath the storeroom and took from there worn-out clothes and worn-out rags and let them down by ropes into the cistern to Jeremiah. Then Ebed-melech the Ethiopian said to Jeremiah, 'Now put these worn-out clothes and rags under your armpits under the ropes'; and Jeremiah did so. So they pulled Jeremiah up with the ropes and lifted him out of the cistern, and Jeremiah stayed in the court of the guardhouse" (Jer. 38:1-13).

Chapter Two

King Zedekiah Sent for Jeremiah the Prophet

"Then King Zedekiah sent and had Jeremiah the prophet brought to him at the third entrance that is in the house of the Lord; and the king said to Jeremiah, 'I am going to ask you something; do not hide anything from me.' Then Jeremiah said to Zedekiah, 'If I tell you, will you not certainly put me to death? Besides, if I give you advice, you will not listen to me.' But King Zedekiah swore to Jeremiah in secret saying, 'As the Lord lives, who made this life for us, surely I will not put you to death nor will I give you over to the hand of these men who are seeking your life'" (Jer. 38:14-16).

Jeremiah the Prophet Prays to the Lord

"Then all the commanders of the forces, Johanan the son of Kareah, Jezaniah the son of Hoshaiah, and all the people both small and great approached and said to Jeremiah the prophet, 'Please let our petition come before you, and pray for us to the Lord your God, that is for all this remnant; because we are left but a few out of many, as your own eyes now see us, that the Lord your God may tell us the way in which we should walk and the thing that we should do.' Then Jeremiah the prophet said to them, 'I have heard you. Behold, I am going to pray to the Lord your God in accordance with your words; and I will tell you the whole message which the Lord will answer you. I will not keep back a word from you.' Then they said to Jeremiah, 'May the Lord be a true and faithful witness against us if we do not act in accordance with the whole message with which the Lord your God will send you to us. Whether it is pleasant or unpleasant, we will listen to the voice of the Lord our God to whom we are sending you, so that it may go well with us when we listen to the voice of the Lord our God'" (Jer. 42:1-6).

The Word of the Lord Came to Jeremiah

"But as soon as Jeremiah, whom the Lord their God had sent, had finished telling all the people all the words of the Lord their God — that is, all these words — Azariah the son of Hoshaiah, and Johanan the son of Kareah, and all the arrogant men said to Jeremiah, 'You are telling a lie! The ord our God has not sent you to say, "You are not to enter Egypt to reside there"; but Baruch the son of Neriah is inciting you against us to give us over into the hand of the Chaldeans, so they will put us to death or exile us to Babylon.' So Johanan the son of Kareah and all the commanders of the forces, and all the people, did not obey the voice of the Lord to stay in the land of Judah. But Johanan the son of Kareah and all the commanders of the forces took the entire remnant of Judah who had returned from all the nations to which they had been driven away, in order to reside in the land of Judah — the men, the women, the children, the king's daughters and every person that Nebuzaradan the captain of the bodyguard had left with Gedaliah the son of Ahikam and grandson of Shaphan, together with Jeremiah the prophet and Baruch the son of Neriah — and they entered the land of Egypt (for they did not obey the voice of the Lord) and went in as far as Tahpanhes. Then the word of the Lord came to Jeremiah in Tahpanhes, saying, 'Take some large stones in your hands and hide them in the mortar in the brick terrace which is at the entrance of Pharaoh's palace in Tahpanhes, in the sight of some of the Jews; and say to them, "Thus says the Lord of hosts, the God of Israel, 'Behold, I am going to send and get Nebuchadnezzar the king of Babylon, My servant, and I am going to set his throne right over these stones that I have hidden; and he will spread his canopy over them. He will also come and strike the land of Egypt; those who are meant for death will be given over to death, and those for captivity to captivity, and those for the sword to the sword. And I shall set fire to the temples of the gods of Egypt, and he will burn them and take them captive. So he will wrap himself with the land of Egypt as a shepherd wraps himself with his garment, and he will depart from there safely. He will also shatter the obelisks of Heliopolis, which is in the land of Egypt; and the temples of the gods of Egypt he will burn with fire'"'" (Jer. 43:1-13).

Jeremiah the Prophet Spoke to Baruch

"This is the message which Jeremiah the prophet spoke to Baruch the son of Neriah, when he had written down these words in a book at Jeremiah's dictation, in the fourth year of Jehoiakim the son of Josiah, king of Judah, saying: 'Thus says the Lord the God of Israel to you, O Baruch: 'You said, 'Ah, woe is me! For the Lord has added sorrow to my pain; I am weary with my groaning and have found no rest.' Thus you are to say to him, "Thus says the Lord, 'Behold, what I have built I am about to tear down, and what I have planted I am about to uproot, that is, the whole land.' But you, are you seeking great things for yourself? Do not seek them; for behold, I am going to bring disaster on all flesh," declares the Lord, "but I will give your life to you as booty in all the places where you may go'" (Jer. 45:1-5).

The Word of the Lord to Jeremiah the Prophet Concerning the Nations

"That which came as the word of the Lord to Jeremiah the prophet concerning the nations. To Egypt, concerning the army of Pharaoh Neco king of Egypt, which was by the Euphrates River at Carchemish, which Nebuchadnezzar king of Babylon defeated in the fourth year of Jehoiakim the son of Josiah, king of Judah: Line up the shield and buckler, And draw near for the battle! Harness the horses, And mount the steeds, And take your stand with helmets on! Polish the spears, Put on the scale-armor! Why have I seen it? They are terrified, They are drawing back, And their mighty men are defeated And have taken refuge in flight, Without facing back; Terror is on every side! Declares the Lord. Let not the swift man flee, Nor the mighty man escape; In the north beside the river Euphrates They have stumbled and fallen. Who is this that rises like the Nile, Like the rivers whose waters surge about? Egypt rises like the Nile, Even like the rivers whose waters surge about; And He has said, 'I will rise and cover that land; I will surely destroy the city and its inhabitants.' Go up, you horses, and drive madly, you chariots, That the mighty men may march forward: Ethiopia and Put, that handle the shield, And the Lydians, that handle and bend the bow. For that day belongs to the Lord God of hosts, A day of vengeance, so as to avenge Himself on His foes; And the sword will devour and be satiated And drink its fill of their blood; For there will be a slaughter for the Lord God of hosts, In the land of the north by the river Euphrates. Go up to Gilead and obtain balm, O virgin daughter of Egypt! In vain have you multiplied remedies; There is no healing for you. The nations have heard of your shame, And the earth is full of your cry of distress; For one warrior has stumbled over another, And both of them have fallen down together" (Jer. 46:1-12).

The Lord Spoke to Jeremiah the Prophet About the Coming of Nebuchadnezzar

"This is the message which the Lord spoke to Jeremiah the prophet about the coming of Nebuchadnezzar king of Babylon to smite the land of Egypt: 'Declare in Egypt and proclaim in Migdol, Proclaim also in Memphis and Tahpanhes; Say, "Take your stand and get yourself ready, For the sword has devoured those around you." Why have your mighty ones become prostrate? They do not stand because the Lord has thrust them down. They have repeatedly stumbled; Indeed, they have fallen one against another. Then they said, "Get up! And let us go back To our own people and our native land Away from the sword of the oppressor." They cried there, "Pharaoh king of Egypt is but a big noise; He has let the appointed time pass by!" As I live,' declares the King Whose name is the Lord of hosts, 'Surely one shall come who looms up like Tabor among the mountains, Or like Carmel by the sea. Make your baggage ready for exile, O daughter dwelling in Egypt, For Memphis will become a desolation; It will even be burned down and bereft of inhabitants. Egypt is a pretty heifer, But a horsefly is coming from the north—it is coming! Also her mercenaries in her midst Are like fattened calves, For even they too have turned back and have fled away together; They did not stand their ground. For the day of their calamity has come upon them, The time of their punishment. Its sound moves along like a serpent; For they move on like an army And come to her as woodcutters with axes. They have cut down her forest,' declares the Lord; 'Surely it will no more be found, Even though they are now more numerous than locusts And are without number. The daughter of Egypt has been put to shame, Given over to the power of the people of the north'" (Jer. 46:13-24).

The Word of the Lord to Jeremiah the Prophet Concerning the Philistines

"That which came as the word of the Lord to Jeremiah the prophet concerning the Philistines, before Pharaoh conquered Gaza. Thus says the Lord: 'Behold, waters are going to rise from the north And become an overflowing torrent, And overflow the land and all its fullness, The city and those who live in it; And the men will cry out, And every inhabitant of the land will wail. Because of the noise of the galloping hoofs of his stallions, The tumult of his chariots, and the rumbling of his wheels, The fathers have not turned back for their children, Because of the limpness of their hands, On account of the day that is coming To destroy all the Philistines, To cut off from Tyre and Sidon Every ally that is left; For the Lord is going to destroy the Philistines, The remnant of the coastland of Caphtor. Baldness has come upon Gaza; Ashkelon has been ruined. O remnant of their valley, How long will you gash yourself? Ah, sword of the Lord, How long will you not be quiet? Withdraw into your sheath; Be at rest and stay still. How can it be quiet, When the Lord has given it an order? Against Ashkelon and against the seacoast—There He has assigned it'" (Jer. 47:1-7).

The Word of the Lord to Jeremiah the Prophet Concerning Elam

"That which came as the word of the Lord to Jeremiah the prophet concerning Elam, at the beginning of the reign of Zedekiah king of Judah, saying: 'Thus says the Lord of hosts, "Behold, I am going to break the bow of Elam, The finest of their might. I will bring upon Elam the four winds From the four ends of heaven, And will scatter them to all these winds; And there will be no nation To which the outcasts of Elam will not go. So I will shatter Elam before their enemies And before those who seek their lives; And I will bring calamity upon them, Even My fierce anger," declares the Lord, "And I will send out the sword after them Until I have consumed them. Then I will set My throne in Elam And destroy out of it king and princes," Declares the Lord. "But it will come about in the last

days That I will restore the fortunes of Elam,'"
Declares the Lord" (Jer. 49:34-39).

A Word Spoken Through Jeremiah the Prophet Concerning Babylon

"The word which the Lord spoke concerning
Babylon, the land of the Chaldeans, through
Jeremiah the prophet: 'Declare and proclaim among
the nations. Proclaim it and lift up a standard. Do
not conceal it but say, "Babylon has been captured,
Bel has been put to shame, Marduk has been
shattered; Her images have been put to shame, her
idols have been shattered.' For a nation has come up
against her out of the north; it will make her land an
object of horror, and there will be no inhabitant in it.
Both man and beast have wandered off, they have
gone away"'" (Jer. 50:1-3)!

The Message Which Jeremiah the Prophet Commanded

"The message which Jeremiah the prophet
commanded Seraiah the son of Neriah, the grandson
of Mahseiah, when he went with Zedekiah the king
of Judah to Babylon in the fourth year of his reign.
(Now Seraiah was quartermaster.) So Jeremiah
wrote in a single scroll all the calamity which would
come upon Babylon, that is, all these words which
have been written concerning Babylon. Then
Jeremiah said to Seraiah, 'As soon as you come to
Babylon, then see that you read all these words
aloud, and say, "You, O Lord, have promised
concerning this place to cut it off, so that there will

be nothing dwelling in it, whether man or beast, but it will be a perpetual desolation." And as soon as you finish reading this scroll, you will tie a stone to it and throw it into the middle of the Euphrates, and say, "Just so shall Babylon sink down and not rise again because of the calamity that I am going to bring upon her; and they will become exhausted.'" Thus far are the words of Jeremiah" (Jer. 51:59-64).

IN THE BOOK OF LAMENTATIONS

Should Priest and Prophet Be Slain in the Sanctuary

"How the Lord has covered the daughter of Zion With a cloud in His anger! He has cast from heaven to earth The glory of Israel, And has not remembered His footstool In the day of His anger. The Lord has swallowed up; He has not spared All the habitations of Jacob. In His wrath He has thrown down The strongholds of the daughter of Judah; He has brought them down to the ground; He has profaned the kingdom and its princes. In fierce anger He has cut off All the strength of Israel; He has drawn back His right hand From before the enemy. And He has burned in Jacob like a flaming fire Consuming round about. He has bent His bow like an enemy; He has set His right hand like an adversary And slain all that were pleasant to the eye; In the tent of the daughter of Zion He has poured out His wrath like fire. The Lord has become like an enemy. He has swallowed up Israel; He has swallowed up all its palaces, He has destroyed its strongholds And multiplied in the daughter of

Chapter Two

Judah Mourning and moaning. And He has violently treated His tabernacle like a garden booth;He has destroyed His appointed meeting place. The Lord has caused to be forgotten The appointed feast and sabbath in Zion, And He has despised king and priest In the indignation of His anger. The Lord has rejected His altar, He has abandoned His sanctuary; He has delivered into the hand of the enemy The walls of her palaces. They have made a noise in the house of the Lord As in the day of an appointed feast. The Lord determined to destroy The wall of the daughter of Zion. He has stretched out a line, He has not restrained His hand from destroying, And He has caused rampart and wall to lament; They have languished together. Her gates have sunk into the ground, He has destroyed and broken her bars. Her king and her princes are among the nations; The law is no more. Also, her prophets find No vision from the Lord. The elders of the daughter of Zion Sit on the ground, they are silent. They have thrown dust on their heads; They have girded themselves with sackcloth. The virgins of Jerusalem Have bowed their heads to the ground. My eyes fail because of tears, My spirit is greatly troubled; My heart is poured out on the earth Because of the destruction of the daughter of my people, When little ones and infants faint In the streets of the city. They say to their mothers, 'Where is grain and wine?' As they faint like a wounded man In the streets of the city, As their life is poured out On their mothers' bosom. How shall I admonish you? To what shall I compare you, O daughter of Jerusalem? To what shall I liken you as I comfort you, O virgin daughter of Zion? For your ruin is as vast as the sea;

Chapter Two

Who can heal you? Your prophets have seen for you False and foolish visions; And they have not exposed your iniquity So as to restore you from captivity, But they have seen for you false and misleading oracles. All who pass along the way Clap their hands in derision at you; They hiss and shake their heads At the daughter of Jerusalem, 'Is this the city of which they said, "The perfection of beauty, A joy to all the earth"?' All your enemies Have opened their mouths wide against you; They hiss and gnash their teeth. They say, 'We have swallowed her up! Surely this is the day for which we waited; We have reached it, we have seen it.' The Lord has done what He purposed; He has accomplished His word Which He commanded from days of old. He has thrown down without sparing, And He has caused the enemy to rejoice over you; He has exalted the might of your adversaries. Their heart cried out to the Lord, 'O wall of the daughter of Zion, Let your tears run down like a river day and night; Give yourself no relief, Let your eyes have no rest. Arise, cry aloud in the night At the beginning of the night watches; Pour out your heart like water Before the presence of the Lord; Lift up your hands to Him For the life of your little ones Who are faint because of hunger At the head of every street.' See, O Lord, and look! With whom have You dealt thus? Should women eat their offspring, The little ones who were born healthy? Should priest and prophet be slain In the sanctuary of the Lord? On the ground in the streets Lie young and old; My virgins and my young men Have fallen by the sword. You have slain them in the day of Your anger, You have slaughtered, not sparing. You called as in the day of an appointed feast My terrors on every side; And there was no one who escaped or survived In the day of the Lord's anger. Those whom I bore and reared, My enemy annihilated them" (La. 2:1-22).

IN THE BOOK OF EZEKIEL

They Will Know that a Prophet Has Been Among Them

"Then He said to me, 'Son of man, stand on your feet that I may speak with you!' As He spoke to me the Spirit entered me and set me on my feet; and I heard Him speaking to me. Then He said to me, 'Son of man, I am sending you to the sons of Israel, to a rebellious people who have rebelled against Me; they and their fathers have transgressed against Me to this very day. I am sending you to them who are stubborn and obstinate children, and you shall say to them, "Thus says the Lord God." As for them, whether they listen or not — for they are a rebellious house — they will know that a prophet has been among them. And you, son of man, neither fear them nor fear their words, though thistles and thorns are with you and you sit on scorpions; neither fear their words nor be dismayed at their presence, for they are a rebellious house. But you shall speak My words to them whether they listen or not, for they are rebellious'" (Eze. 2:1-7).

They Will Seek a Vision from a Prophet

"Make the chain, for the land is full of bloody crimes and the city is full of violence. Therefore, I will bring the worst of the nations, and they will possess their houses. I will also make the pride of the strong ones cease, and their holy places will be profaned. When anguish comes, they will seek peace, but there will be none. Disaster will come upon disaster and rumor will be added to rumor; then they will seek a vision from a prophet, but the law will be lost from the priest and counsel from the elders. The king will mourn, the prince will be clothed with horror, and the hands of the people of the land will tremble. According to their conduct I will deal with them, and by their judgments I will judge them. And they will know that I am the Lord" (Eze. 7:23-27).

To the Prophet

"Then some elders of Israel came to me and sat down before me. And the word of the Lord came to me, saying, Son of man, these men have set up their idols in their hearts and have put right before their faces the stumbling block of their iniquity. Should I be consulted by them at all? Therefore speak to them and tell them, 'Thus says the Lord God, "Any man of the house of Israel who sets up his idols in his heart, puts right before his face the stumbling block of his iniquity, and then comes to the prophet, I the Lord will be brought to give him an answer in the matter in view of the multitude of his idols, in order to lay hold of the hearts of the house of Israel who are estranged from Me through all their idols"'" (Eze. 14:1-5).

Chapter Two

Comes to the Prophet to Inquire of Me

"Therefore say to the house of Israel, 'Thus says the Lord God, "Repent and turn away from your idols and turn your faces away from all your abominations. For anyone of the house of Israel or of the immigrants who stay in Israel who separates himself from Me, sets up his idols in his heart, puts right before his face the stumbling block of his iniquity, and then comes to the prophet to inquire of Me for himself, I the Lord will be brought to answer him in My own person. I will set My face against that man and make him a sign and a proverb, and I will cut him off from among My people. So you will know that I am the Lord"'" (Eze. 14:6-8).

If the Prophet Is Prevailed Upon

"But if the prophet is prevailed upon to speak a word, it is I, the Lord, who have prevailed upon that prophet, and I will stretch out My hand against him and destroy him from among My people Israel. They will bear the punishment of their iniquity; as the iniquity of the inquirer is, so the iniquity of the prophet will be, in order that the house of Israel may no longer stray from Me and no longer defile themselves with all their transgressions. Thus they will be My people, and I shall be their God,' declares the Lord God" (Eze. 14:9-11).

A Prophet Has Been in Their Midst

"'But as for you, son of man, your fellow citizens who talk about you by the walls and in the doorways of the houses, speak to one another, each to his brother, saying, 'Come now and hear what the message is which comes forth from the Lord.' They come to you as people come, and sit before you as My people and hear your words, but they do not do them, for they do the lustful desires expressed by their mouth, and their heart goes after their gain. Behold, you are to them like a sensual song by one who has a beautiful voice and plays well on an instrument; for they hear your words but they do not practice them. So when it comes to pass — as surely it will — then they will know that a prophet has been in their midst" (Eze. 33:30-33).

IN THE BOOK OF DANIEL

The Word of the Lord to Jeremiah the Prophet

"In the first year of Darius the son of Ahasuerus, of Median descent, who was made king over the kingdom of the Chaldeans — in the first year of his reign, I, Daniel, observed in the books the number of the years which was revealed as the word of the Lord to Jeremiah the prophet for the completion of the desolations of Jerusalem, namely, seventy years. So I gave my attention to the Lord God to seek Him by prayer and supplications, with fasting, sackcloth and ashes. I prayed to the Lord my God and confessed and said, 'Alas, O Lord, the great and awesome God, who keeps His covenant and lovingkindness for those who love Him and keep His commandments, we have sinned, committed iniquity, acted wickedly and rebelled, even turning aside from Your commandments and ordinances.

Chapter Two

Moreover, we have not listened to Your servants the prophets, who spoke in Your name to our kings, our princes, our fathers and all the people of the land'" (Da. 9:1-6).

IN THE BOOK OF HOSEA

The Prophet Also Will Stumble with You

"Yet let no one find fault, and let none offer reproof; For your people are like those who contend with the priest. So you will stumble by day, And the prophet also will stumble with you by night; And I will destroy your mother. My people are destroyed for lack of knowledge. Because you have rejected knowledge, I also will reject you from being My priest. Since you have forgotten the law of your God, I also will forget your children" (Hos. 4:4-6).

The Prophet Is a Fool

"The days of punishment have come, The days of retribution have come; Let Israel know this! The prophet is a fool, The inspired man is demented, Because of the grossness of your iniquity, And because your hostility is so great. Ephraim was a watchman with my God, a prophet; Yet the snare of a bird catcher is in all his ways, And there is only hostility in the house of his God. They have gone deep in depravity As in the days of Gibeah; He will remember their iniquity, He will punish their sins" (Hos. 9:7-9).

Chapter Two

By a Prophet He Was Kept

"Now Jacob fled to the land of Aram, And Israel worked for a wife, And for a wife he kept sheep. But by a prophet the Lord brought Israel from Egypt, And by a prophet he was kept. Ephraim has provoked to bitter anger; So his Lord will leave his bloodguilt on him And bring back his reproach to him" (Hos. 12:12-14).

IN THE BOOK OF AMOS

I Am Not a Prophet, For I Am a Herdsman and a Grower of Sycamore Figs

"Then Amos replied to Amaziah, 'I am not a prophet, nor am I the son of a prophet; for I am a herdsman and a grower of sycamore figs. But the Lord took me from following the flock and the Lord said to me, "Go prophesy to My people Israel." Now hear the word of the Lord: you are saying, "You shall not prophesy against Israel nor shall you speak against the house of Isaac." Therefore, thus says the Lord, "Your wife will become a harlot in the city, your sons and your daughters will fall by the sword, your land will be parceled up by a measuring line and you yourself will die upon unclean soil. Moreover, Israel will certainly go from its land into exile'" (Am. 7:14-17).

Chapter Two

IN THE BOOK OF HABAKKUK

The Oracle Which Habakkuk the Prophet Saw

"The oracle which Habakkuk the prophet saw. How long, O Lord, will I call for help, And You will not hear? I cry out to You, 'Violence!' Yet You do not save. Why do You make me see iniquity, And cause me to look on wickedness? Yes, destruction and violence are before me; Strife exists and contention arises. Therefore the law is ignored And justice is never upheld. For the wicked surround the righteous; Therefore justice comes out perverted" (Hab. 1:1-4).

A Prayer of Habakkuk the Prophet

"A prayer of Habakkuk the prophet, according to Shigionoth. Lord, I have heard the report about You and I fear. O Lord, revive Your work in the midst of the years, In the midst of the years make it known; In wrath remember mercy" (Hab. 3:1-2).

IN THE BOOK OF HAGGAI

The Word of the Lord Came by the Prophet Haggai

"In the second year of Darius the king, on the first day of the sixth month, the word of the Lord came by the prophet Haggai to Zerubbabel the son of Shealtiel, governor of Judah, and to Joshua the son of Jehozadak, the high priest, saying, 'Thus says the Lord of hosts, "This people says, 'The time has not come, even the time for the house of the Lord to be rebuilt.'''' Then the word of the Lord came by Haggai the prophet, saying, 'Is it time for you yourselves to dwell in your paneled houses while this house lies desolate?' Now therefore, thus says the Lord of hosts, 'Consider your ways! You have sown much, but harvest little; you eat, but there is not enough to be satisfied; you drink, but there is not enough to become drunk; you put on clothing, but no one is warm enough;and he who earns, earns wages to put into a purse with holes'" (Hag. 1:1-6).

The Words of Haggai the Prophet

"'Then Zerubbabel the son of Shealtiel, and Joshua the son of Jehozadak, the high priest, with all the remnant of the people, obeyed the voice of the Lord their God and the words of Haggai the prophet, as the Lord their God had sent him. And the people showed reverence for the Lord. Then Haggai, the messenger of the Lord, spoke by the commission of the Lord to the people saying, "I am with you," declares the Lord.' So the Lord stirred up the spirit of Zerubbabel the son of Shealtiel, governor of Judah, and the spirit of Joshua the son of Jehozadak, the high priest, and the spirit of all the remnant of the people; and they came and worked on the house of the Lord of hosts, their God, on the twenty-fourth day of the sixth month in the second year of Darius the king" (Hag. 1:12-15).

Chapter Two

The Word of the Lord Came by the Prophet Haggai

"On the twenty-first of the seventh month, the word of the Lord came by Haggai the prophet saying, 'Speak now to Zerubbabel the son of Shealtiel, governor of Judah, and to Joshua the son of Jehozadak, the high priest, and to the remnant of the people saying, "Who is left among you who saw this temple in its former glory? And how do you see it now? Does it not seem to you like nothing in comparison? But now take courage, Zerubbabel," declares the Lord, "take courage also, Joshua son of Jehozadak, the high priest, and all you people of the land take courage," declares the Lord, "and work; for I am with you," declares the Lord of hosts. "As for the promise which I made you when you came out of Egypt, My Spirit is abiding in your midst; do not fear!" For thus says the Lord of hosts, "Once more in a little while, I am going to shake the heavens and the earth, the sea also and the dry land. I will shake all the nations; and they will come with the wealth of all nations, and I will fill this house with glory," says the Lord of hosts. "The silver is Mine and the gold is Mine," declares the Lord of hosts. "The latter glory of this house will be greater than the former," says the Lord of hosts, "and in this place I will give peace," declares the Lord of hosts.' On the twenty-fourth of the ninth month, in the second year of Darius, the word of the Lord came to Haggai the prophet, saying, 'Thus says the Lord of hosts, 'Ask now the priests for a ruling: 'If a man carries holy meat in the fold of his garment, and touches bread with this fold, or cooked food, wine, oil, or any other food, will it become holy?'" And the priests answered, 'No.' Then Haggai said, 'If one who is unclean from a corpse touches any of these, will the latter become unclean?' And the priests answered, 'It will become unclean.' Then Haggai said, "'So is this people. And so is this nation before Me," declares the Lord, "and so is every work of their hands; and what they offer there is unclean. But now, do consider from this day onward: before one stone was placed on another in the temple of the Lord, from that time when one came to a grain heap of twenty measures, there would be only ten; and when one came to the wine vat to draw fifty measures, there would be only twenty. I smote you and every work of your hands with blasting wind, mildew and hail; yet you did not come back to Me," declares the Lord. "Do consider from this day onward, from the twenty-fourth day of the ninth month;from the day when the temple of the Lord was founded, consider: Is the seed still in the barn? Even including the vine, the fig tree, the pomegranate and the olive tree, it has not borne fruit. Yet from this day on I will bless you.'"" (Hag. 2:1-19).

IN THE BOOK OF ZECHARIAH

The Word of the Lord Came to Zechariah the Prophet

"In the eighth month of the second year of Darius, the word of the Lord came to Zechariah the prophet, the son of Berechiah, the son of Iddo saying, 'The Lord was very angry with your fathers. Therefore say to them, "Thus says the Lord of hosts,

'Return to Me,' declares the Lord of hosts, 'that I may return to you,' says the Lord of hosts. Do not be like your fathers, to whom the former prophets proclaimed, saying, "Thus says the Lord of hosts, 'Return now from your evil ways and from your evil deeds.'" But they did not listen or give heed to Me,' declares the Lord. 'Your fathers, where are they? And the prophets, do they live forever? But did not My words and My statutes, which I commanded My servants the prophets, overtake your fathers? Then they repented and said, "As the Lord of hosts purposed to do to us in accordance with our ways and our deeds, so He has dealt with us.'"'" On the twenty-fourth day of the eleventh month, which is the month Shebat, in the second year of Darius, the word of the Lord came to Zechariah the prophet, the son of Berechiah, the son of Iddo, as follows: I saw at night, and behold, a man was riding on a red horse, and he was standing among the myrtle trees which were in the ravine, with red, sorrel and white horses behind him. Then I said, 'My lord, what are these?' And the angel who was speaking with me said to me, 'I will show you what these are.' And the man who was standing among the myrtle trees answered and said, 'These are those whom the Lord has sent to patrol the earth.' So they answered the angel of the Lord who was standing" (Zec. 1:1-11).

I Am Not a Prophet; I Am a Tiller of the Ground

"'It will come about in that day,' declares the Lord of hosts, 'that I will cut off the names of the idols from the land, and they will no longer be remembered; and I will also remove the prophets and the unclean spirit from the land. And if anyone still prophesies, then his father and mother who gave birth to him will say to him, "You shall not live, for you have spoken falsely in the name of the Lord"; and his father and mother who gave birth to him will pierce him through when he prophesies. Also it will come about in that day that the prophets will each be ashamed of his vision when he prophesies, and they will not put on a hairy robe in order to deceive; but he will say, "I am not a prophet; I am a tiller of the ground, for a man sold me as a slave in my youth." And one will say to him, "What are these wounds between your arms?" Then he will say, "Those with which I was wounded in the house of my friends"'" (Zec. 13:2-6).

IN THE BOOK OF MALACHI

I Am Going to Send You Elijah the Prophet

"Behold, I am going to send you Elijah the prophet before the coming of the great and terrible day of the Lord. He will restore the hearts of the fathers to their children and the hearts of the children to their fathers, so that I will not come and smite the land with a curse" (Mal. 4:5-6).

Chapter Three

PROPHETS IN THE NEW TESTAMENT

IN THE BOOK OF MATTHEW

By the Lord through the Prophet Might be Fulfilled

"Now the birth of Jesus Christ was as follows: when His mother Mary had been betrothed to Joseph, before they came together she was found to be with child by the Holy Spirit. And Joseph her husband, being a righteous man and not wanting to disgrace her, planned to send her away secretly. But when he had considered this, behold, an angel of the Lord appeared to him in a dream, saying, 'Joseph, son of David, do not be afraid to take Mary as your wife; for the Child who has been conceived in her is of the Holy Spirit. She will bear a Son; and you shall call His name Jesus, for He will save His people from their sins.' Now all this took place to fulfill what was spoken by the Lord through the prophet: 'BEHOLD, THE VIRGIN SHALL BE WITH CHILD AND SHALL BEAR A SON, AND THEY SHALL CALL HIS NAME IMMANUEL,' which translated means, 'GOD WITH US.' And Joseph awoke from his sleep and did as the angel of the Lord commanded him, and took Mary as his wife, but kept her a virgin until she gave birth to a Son; and he called His name Jesus" (Mt. 1:18-25).

It Has Been Written by the Prophet

"Now after Jesus was born in Bethlehem of Judea in the days of Herod the king, magi from the east arrived in Jerusalem, saying, 'Where is He who has been born King of the Jews? For we saw His star in the east and have come to worship Him.' When Herod the king heard this, he was troubled, and all Jerusalem with him. Gathering together all the chief priests and scribes of the people, he inquired of them where the Messiah was to be born. They said to him, 'In Bethlehem of Judea; for this is what has been written by the prophet: "AND YOU, BETHLEHEM, LAND OF JUDAH, ARE BY NO MEANS LEAST AMONG THE LEADERS OF JUDAH; FOR OUT OF YOU SHALL COME FORTH A RULER WHO WILL SHEPHERD MY PEOPLE ISRAEL'"" (Mt. 2:1-6).

Spoken by the Lord Through the Prophet

"So Joseph got up and took the Child and His mother while it was still night, and left for Egypt. He remained there until the death of Herod. This was to fulfill what had been spoken by the Lord through the prophet: 'OUT OF EGYPT I CALLED MY SON'" (Mt. 2:14-15).

Spoken Through Jeremiah the Prophet Was Fulfilled

"Then when Herod saw that he had been tricked by the magi, he became very enraged, and sent and slew all the male children who were in Bethlehem and all its vicinity, from two years old and under, according to the time which he had determined from the magi. Then what had been spoken through Jeremiah the prophet was fulfilled: 'A VOICE WAS HEARD IN RAMAH, WEEPING AND GREAT MOURNING, RACHEL WEEPING FOR HER CHILDREN; AND SHE REFUSED TO BE COMFORTED, BECAUSE THEY WERE NO MORE'" (Mt. 2:16-18).

This Is the One Referred to by Isaiah the Prophet

"Now in those days John the Baptist *came, preaching in the wilderness of Judea, saying, 'Repent, for the kingdom of heaven is at hand. For this is the one referred to by Isaiah the prophet when he said, "THE VOICE OF ONE CRYING IN THE WILDERNESS, 'MAKE READY THE WAY OF THE LORD, MAKE HIS PATHS STRAIGHT!'" Now John himself had a garment of camel's hair and a leather belt around his waist; and his food was locusts and wild honey. Then Jerusalem was going out to him, and all Judea and all the district around the Jordan; and they were being baptized by him in the Jordan River, as they confessed their sins" (Mt. 3:1-6).

Isaiah the Prophet

"Now when Jesus heard that John had been taken into custody, He withdrew into Galilee; and leaving Nazareth, He came and settled in Capernaum, which is by the sea, in the region of Zebulun and Naphtali. This was to fulfill what was spoken through Isaiah the prophet: 'THE LAND OF ZEBULUN AND THE LAND OF NAPHTALI, BY THE WAY OF THE SEA, BEYOND THE JORDAN, GALILEE OF THE GENTILES—THE PEOPLE WHO WERE SITTING IN DARKNESS SAW A GREAT LIGHT, AND THOSE WHO WERE SITTING IN THE LAND AND SHADOW OF DEATH, UPON THEM A LIGHT DAWNED'" (Mt. 4:12-16).

Through Isaiah the Prophet

"When Jesus came into Peter's home, He saw his mother-in-law lying sick in bed with a fever. He touched her hand, and the fever left her; and she got up and waited on Him. When evening came, they brought to Him many who were demon-possessed; and He cast out the spirits with a word, and healed all who were ill. This was to fulfill what was spoken through Isaiah the prophet: 'HE

Chapter Three

HIMSELF TOOK OUR INFIRMITIES AND CARRIED AWAY OUR DISEASES'" (Mt. 8:14-17).

He Who Receives a Prophet Shall Receive a Prophet's Reward

"He who receives you receives Me, and he who receives Me receives Him who sent Me. He who receives a prophet in the name of a prophet shall receive a prophet's reward; and he who receives a righteous man in the name of a righteous man shall receive a righteous man's reward. And whoever in the name of a disciple gives to one of these little ones even a cup of cold water to drink, truly I say to you, he shall not lose his reward" (Mt. 10:40-42).

Why Did You Go Out? To See a Prophet?

"As these men were going away, Jesus began to speak to the crowds about John, 'What did you go out into the wilderness to see? A reed shaken by the wind? But what did you go out to see? A man dressed in soft clothing? Those who wear soft clothing are in kings' palaces! But what did you go out to see? A prophet? Yes, I tell you, and one who is more than a prophet. This is the one about whom it is written, "BEHOLD, I SEND MY MESSENGER AHEAD OF YOU, WHO WILL PREPARE YOUR WAY BEFORE YOU." Truly I say to you, among those born of women there has not arisen anyone greater than John the Baptist! Yet the one who is least in the kingdom of heaven is greater than he. From the days of John the Baptist until now the kingdom of heaven suffers violence, and violent men take it by force. For all the prophets and the Law prophesied until John And if you are willing to accept it, John himself is Elijah who was to come. He who has ears to hear, let him hear'" (Mt. 11:7-15).

Chapter Three

Through Isaiah the Prophet, Might be Fulfilled

"But Jesus, aware of this, withdrew from there. Many followed Him, and He healed them all, and warned them not to tell who He was. This was to fulfill what was spoken through Isaiah the prophet: 'BEHOLD, MY SERVANT WHOM I HAVE CHOSEN; MY BELOVED IN WHOM MY SOUL is WELL-PLEASED; I WILL PUT MY SPIRIT UPON HIM, AND HE SHALL PROCLAIM JUSTICE TO THE GENTILES. HE WILL NOT QUARREL, NOR CRY OUT; NOR WILL ANYONE HEAR HIS VOICE IN THE STREETS. A BATTERED REED HE WILL NOT BREAK OFF, AND A SMOLDERING WICK HE WILL NOT PUT OUT, UNTIL HE LEADS JUSTICE TO VICTORY. AND IN HIS NAME THE GENTILES WILL HOPE'" (Mt. 12:15-21).

The Sign of Jonah the Prophet

"Then some of the scribes and Pharisees said to Him, 'Teacher, we want to see a sign from You.' But He answered and said to them, 'An evil and adulterous generation craves for a sign; and yet no sign will be given to it but the sign of Jonah the prophet; for just as JONAH WAS THREE DAYS AND THREE NIGHTS IN THE BELLY OF THE SEA MONSTER, so will the Son of Man be three days and three nights in the heart of the earth. The men of Nineveh will stand up with this generation at the judgment, and will condemn it because they repented at the preaching of Jonah; and behold, something greater than Jonah is here. The Queen of the South will rise up with this generation at the judgment and will condemn it, because she came from the ends of the earth to hear the wisdom of Solomon; and behold, something greater than Solomon is here" (Mt. 12:38-42).

Chapter Three

Through the Prophet

"Then He left the crowds and went into the house. And His disciples came to Him and said, 'Explain to us the parable of the tares of the field.' And He said, 'The one who sows the good seed is the Son of Man, and the field is the world; and as for the good seed, these are the sons of the kingdom; and the tares are the sons of the evil one; and the enemy who sowed them is the devil, and the harvest is the end of the age; and the reapers are angels. So just as the tares are gathered up and burned with fire, so shall it be at the end of the age. The Son of Man will send forth His angels, and they will gather out of His kingdom all stumbling blocks, and those who commit lawlessness'" (Mt. 13:36-41).

A Prophet Is Not Without Honor Except in His Home Town, and in His Own Household

"When Jesus had finished these parables, He departed from there. He came to His hometown and began teaching them in their synagogue, so that they were astonished, and said, 'Where did this man get this wisdom and these miraculous powers? Is not this the carpenter's son? Is not His mother called Mary, and His brothers, James and Joseph and Simon and Judas? And His sisters, are they not all with us? Where then did this man get all these things?' And they took offense at Him. But Jesus said to them, 'A prophet is not without honor except in his hometown and in his own household.' And He did not do many miracles there because of their unbelief" (Mt. 13:53-58).

Chapter Three

They Regarded Him as a Prophet.

"For when Herod had John arrested, he bound him and put him in prison because of Herodias, the wife of his brother Philip. For John had been saying to him, 'It is not lawful for you to have her.' Although Herod wanted to put him to death, he feared the crowd, because they regarded John as a prophet" (Mt. 14:3-5).

This Is the Prophet Jesus, from Nazareth in Galilee

"When they had approached Jerusalem and had come to Bethphage, at the Mount of Olives, then Jesus sent two disciples, saying to them, 'Go into the village opposite you, and immediately you will find a donkey tied there and a colt with her; untie them and bring them to Me. If anyone says anything to you, you shall say, "The Lord has need of them," and immediately he will send them.' This took place to fulfill what was spoken through the prophet: 'SAY TO THE DAUGHTER OF ZION, "BEHOLD YOUR KING IS COMING TO YOU, GENTLE, AND MOUNTED ON A DONKEY, EVEN ON A COLT, THE FOAL OF A BEAST OF BURDEN."' The disciples went and did just as Jesus had instructed them, and brought the donkey and the colt, and laid their coats on them; and He sat on the coats. Most of the crowd spread their coats in the road, and others were cutting branches from the trees and spreading them in the road. The crowds going ahead of Him, and those who followed, were shouting, 'Hosanna to the Son of David; BLESSED IS HE WHO COMES IN THE NAME OF THE LORD; Hosanna in the highest!' When He had entered Jerusalem, all the city was stirred, saying, 'Who is this?' And the crowds were saying, 'This is the prophet Jesus, from Nazareth in Galilee'" (Mt. 21:1-11).

Chapter Three

They All Hold John to be a Prophet

"When He entered the temple, the chief priests and the elders of the people came to Him while He was teaching, and said, 'By what authority are You doing these things, and who gave You this authority?' Jesus said to them, 'I will also ask you one thing, which if you tell Me, I will also tell you by what authority I do these things. The baptism of John was from what source, from heaven or from men?' And they began reasoning among themselves, saying, 'If we say, "From heaven," He will say to us, "Then why did you not believe him?" But if we say, "From men," we fear the people; for they all regard John as a prophet.' And answering Jesus, they said, 'We do not know.' He also said to them, 'Neither will I tell you by what authority I do these things'" (Mt. 21:23-27).

They Held Him to Be a Prophet.

"When the chief priests and the Pharisees heard His parables, they understood that He was speaking about them. When they sought to seize Him, they feared the people, because they considered Him to be a prophet" (Mt. 21:45-46).

Which Was Spoken of Through Daniel the Prophet

"Therefore when you see the ABOMINATION OF DESOLATION which was spoken of through Daniel the prophet, standing in the holy place (let the reader understand), then those who are in Judea must flee to the mountains. Whoever is on the housetop must not go down to get the things out that are in his house. Whoever is in the field must not turn back to get his cloak. But woe to those who are pregnant and to those who are nursing babies in those days! But pray that your flight will not be in the winter, or on a Sabbath. For then there will be a great tribulation, such as has not occurred since the beginning of the world until now, nor ever will. Unless those days had been cut short, no life would have been saved; but for the sake of the elect those days will be cut short. Then if anyone says to you, 'Behold, here is the Christ,' or 'There He is,' do not believe him. For false Christs and false prophets will arise and will show great signs and wonders, so as to mislead, if possible, even the elect. Behold, I have told you in advance. So if they say to you, 'Behold, He is in the wilderness,' do not go out, or, 'Behold, He is in the inner rooms,' do not believe them. For just as the lightning comes from the east and flashes even to the west, so will the coming of the Son of Man be. Wherever the corpse is, there the vultures will gather" (Mt. 24:15-28).

Spoken Through Jeremiah the Prophet

"Then when Judas, who had betrayed Him, saw that He had been condemned, he felt remorse and returned the thirty pieces of silver to the chief priests and elders, saying, 'I have sinned by betraying innocent blood.' But they said, 'What is that to us? See to that yourself!' And he threw the pieces of silver into the temple sanctuary and departed; and he went away and hanged himself. The chief priests took the pieces of silver and said, 'It is not lawful to put them into the temple treasury, since it is the price of blood.' And they conferred together and with the money bought the Potter's Field as a burial place for strangers. For this reason that field has been called the Field of Blood to this day. Then that which was spoken through Jeremiah the prophet was fulfilled: 'AND THEY TOOK THE THIRTY PIECES OF SILVER, THE PRICE OF

Chapter Three

THE ONE WHOSE PRICE HAD BEEN SET by the sons of Israel; AND THEY GAVE THEM FOR THE POTTER'S FIELD, AS THE LORD DIRECTED ME'" (Mt. 27:3-10).

IN THE BOOK OF MARK

It Is Written in Isaiah the Prophet

"As it is written in Isaiah the prophet: 'BEHOLD, I SEND MY MESSENGER AHEAD OF YOU, WHO WILL PREPARE YOUR WAY; THE VOICE OF ONE CRYING IN THE WILDERNESS, "MAKE READY THE WAY OF THE LORD, MAKE HIS PATHS STRAIGHT.'" John the Baptist appeared in the wilderness preaching a baptism of repentance for the forgiveness of sins. And all the country of Judea was going out to him, and all the people of Jerusalem; and they were being baptized by him in the Jordan River, confessing their sins. John was clothed with camel's hair and wore a leather belt around his waist, and his diet was locusts and wild honey. And he was preaching, and saying, 'After me One is coming who is mightier than I, and I am not fit to stoop down and untie the thong of His sandals. I baptized you with water; but He will baptize you with the Holy Spirit'" (Mk. 1:2-8).

A Prophet Is Not Without Honor

"Jesus went out from there and came into His hometown; and His disciples *followed Him. When the Sabbath came, He began to teach in the synagogue; and the many listeners were astonished, saying, 'Where did this man get these things, and what is this wisdom given to Him, and such miracles as these performed by His hands? Is not this the carpenter, the son of Mary, and brother of James and Joses and Judas and Simon? Are not His sisters here with us?' And they took offense at Him. Jesus said to them, 'A prophet is not without honor except in his hometown and among his own relatives and in his own household.' And He could do no miracle there except that He laid His hands on a few sick people and healed them. And He wondered at their unbelief. And He was going around the villages teaching" (Mk. 6:1-6).

He Is a Prophet, Like One of the Prophets of Old

"And King Herod heard of it, for His name had become well known; and people were saying, 'John the Baptist has risen from the dead, and that is why these miraculous powers are at work in Him.' But others were saying, 'He is Elijah.' And others were saying, 'He is a prophet, like one of the prophets of old.' But when Herod heard of it, he kept saying, 'John, whom I beheaded, has risen!'" (Mk. 6:14-16).

All Considered John to Have Been a Prophet Indeed

"They came again to Jerusalem. And as He was walking in the temple, the chief priests and the scribes and the elders came to Him, and began saying to Him, 'By what authority are You doing these things, or who gave You this authority to do these things?' And Jesus said to them, 'I will ask you one question, and you answer Me, and then I will tell you by what authority I do these things. Was the baptism of John from heaven, or from men? Answer Me.' They began reasoning among themselves, saying, 'If we say, "From heaven," He will say, "Then why did you not believe him?" But shall we say, "From men"?' —they were afraid of the people, for everyone considered John to have been a real prophet. Answering Jesus, they said, 'We do not know.' And Jesus said to them, 'Nor will I tell you by what authority I do these things'" (Mk. 11:27-33).

IN THE BOOK OF LUKE

And You, Child, Will Be Called the Prophet of the Most High

"And his father Zacharias was filled with the Holy Spirit, and prophesied, saying: 'Blessed be the Lord God of Israel, For He has visited us and accomplished redemption for His people, And has raised up a horn of salvation for us In the house of David His servant — As He spoke by the mouth of His holy prophets from of old — Salvation FROM OUR ENEMIES, And FROM THE HAND OF ALL WHO HATE US; To show mercy toward our fathers, And to remember His holy covenant, The oath which He swore to Abraham our father, To grant us that we, being rescued from the hand of our enemies, Might serve Him without fear, In holiness and righteousness before Him all our days. And you, child, will be called the prophet of the Most High; For you will go on BEFORE THE LORD TO PREPARE HIS WAYS; To give to His people the knowledge of salvation By the forgiveness of their sins, Because of the tender mercy of our God, With which the Sunrise from on high will visit us, TO SHINE UPON THOSE WHO SIT IN DARKNESS AND THE SHADOW OF DEATH, To guide our feet into the way of peace'" (Lk. 1:67-79).

Isaiah the Prophet

"Now in the fifteenth year of the reign of Tiberius Caesar, when Pontius Pilate was governor of Judea, and Herod was tetrarch of Galilee, and his brother Philip was tetrarch of the region of Ituraea and Trachonitis, and

Chapter Three

Lysanias was tetrarch of Abilene, in the high priesthood of Annas and Caiaphas, the word of God came to John, the son of Zacharias, in the wilderness. And he came into all the district around the Jordan, preaching a baptism of repentance for the forgiveness of sins; as it is written in the book of the words of Isaiah the prophet, 'THE VOICE OF ONE CRYING IN THE WILDERNESS, "MAKE READY THE WAY OF THE LORD, MAKE HIS PATHS STRAIGHT. 'EVERY RAVINE WILL BE FILLED, AND EVERY MOUNTAIN AND HILL WILL BE BROUGHT LOW; THE CROOKED WILL BECOME STRAIGHT, AND THE ROUGH ROADS SMOOTH; AND ALL FLESH WILL SEE THE SALVATION OF GOD"'" (Lk. 3:1-6).

The Book of the Prophet Isaiah Was Handed to Him

"And Jesus returned to Galilee in the power of the Spirit, and news about Him spread through all the surrounding district. And He began teaching in their synagogues and was praised by all. And He came to Nazareth, where He had been brought up; and as was His custom, He entered the synagogue on the Sabbath, and stood up to read. And the book of the prophet Isaiah was handed to Him. And He opened the book and found the place where it was written, 'THE SPIRIT OF THE LORD IS UPON ME, BECAUSE HE ANOINTED ME TO PREACH THE GOSPEL TO THE POOR. HE HAS SENT ME TO PROCLAIM RELEASE TO THE CAPTIVES, AND RECOVERY OF SIGHT TO THE BLIND, TO SET FREE THOSE WHO ARE OPPRESSED, TO PROCLAIM THE FAVORABLE YEAR OF THE LORD.' And He closed the book, gave it back to the attendant and sat down; and the eyes of all in the synagogue were fixed on Him. And He began to say to them, 'Today this Scripture has been fulfilled in your hearing.' And all were speaking well of

Him, and wondering at the gracious words which were falling from His lips; and they were saying, 'Is this not Joseph's son?' And He said to them, 'No doubt you will quote this proverb to Me, "Physician, heal yourself! Whatever we heard was done at Capernaum, do here in your hometown as well."' And He said, 'Truly I say to you, no prophet is welcome in his hometown. But I say to you in truth, there were many widows in Israel in the days of Elijah, when the sky was shut up for three years and six months, when a great famine came over all the land; and yet Elijah was sent to none of them, but only to Zarephath, in the land of Sidon, to a woman who was a widow. And there were many lepers in Israel in the time of Elisha the prophet; and none of them was cleansed, but only Naaman the Syrian.' And all the people in the synagogue were filled with rage as they heard these things; and they got up and drove Him out of the city, and led Him to the brow of the hill on which their city had been built. in order to throw Him down the cliff. But passing through their midst, He went His way" (Lk. 4:14-30).

A Great Prophet Has Arisen Among Us

"Soon afterwards He went to a city called Nain; and His disciples were going along with Him, accompanied by a large crowd. Now as He approached the gate of the city, a dead man was being carried out, the only son of his mother, and she was a widow; and a sizeable crowd from the city was with her. When the Lord saw her, He felt compassion for her, and said to her, 'Do not weep.' And He came up and touched the coffin; and the bearers came to a halt. And He said, 'Young man, I say to you, arise!' The dead man sat up and began to speak. And Jesus gave him back to his mother. Fear gripped them all, and they began glorifying God, saying, 'A great prophet has arisen among us!' and, 'God has visited His people!' This report concerning Him went out all over Judea and in all the surrounding district" (Lk. 7:11-17).

One Who Is More Than a Prophet

"When the messengers of John had left, He began to speak to the crowds about John, 'What did you go out into the wilderness to see? A reed shaken by the wind? But what did you go out to see? A man dressed in soft clothing? Those who are splendidly clothed and live in luxury are found in royal palaces! But what did you go out to see? A prophet? Yes, I say to you, and one who is more than a prophet. This is the one about whom it is written, "BEHOLD, I SEND MY MESSENGER AHEAD OF YOU, WHO WILL PREPARE YOUR WAY BEFORE YOU." I say to you, among those born of women there is no one greater than John; yet he who is least in the kingdom of God is greater than he.' When all the people and the tax collectors heard this, they acknowledged God's justice, having been baptized with the baptism of John. But the Pharisees and the lawyers rejected God's purpose for themselves, not having been baptized by John" (Lk. 7:24-30).

If This Man Were a Prophet

"Now one of the Pharisees was requesting Him to dine with him, and He entered the Pharisee's house and reclined at the table. And there was a woman in the city who was a sinner; and when she learned that He was reclining at the table in the Pharisee's house, she brought an alabaster vial of perfume, and standing behind Him at His feet, weeping, she began to wet His feet with her tears, and kept wiping them with the hair of her head, and kissing His feet and anointing them with the perfume.

Chapter Three

Now when the Pharisee who had invited Him saw this, he said to himself, 'If this man were a prophet He would know who and what sort of person this woman is who is touching Him, that she is a sinner.' And Jesus answered him, 'Simon, I have something to say to you.' And he replied, 'Say it, Teacher.' A moneylender had two debtors: one owed five hundred denarii, and the other fifty. When they were unable to repay, he graciously forgave them both. So which of them will love him more?' Simon answered and said, 'I suppose the one whom he forgave more.' And He said to him, 'You have judged correctly.' Turning toward the woman, He said to Simon, 'Do you see this woman? I entered your house; you gave Me no water for My feet, but she has wet My feet with her tears and wiped them with her hair. You gave Me no kiss; but she, since the time I came in, has not ceased to kiss My feet. You did not anoint My head with oil, but she anointed My feet with perfume. For this reason I say to you, her sins, which are many, have been forgiven, for she loved much; but he who is forgiven little, loves little.' Then He said to her, 'Your sins have been forgiven.' Those who were reclining at the table with Him began to say to themselves, 'Who is this man who even forgives sins?' And He said to the woman, 'Your faith has saved you; go in peace'" (Lk. 7:36-50).

That a Prophet Should Perish Outside of Jerusalem

"Just at that time some Pharisees approached, saying to Him, 'Go away, leave here, for Herod wants to kill You.' And He said to them, 'Go and tell that fox, "Behold, I cast out demons and perform cures today and tomorrow, and the third day I reach My goal." Nevertheless I must journey on today and tomorrow and the next day; for it cannot be that a prophet would perish outside of Jerusalem. O Jerusalem, Jerusalem, the city that kills the prophets and stones those sent to her! How often I wanted to gather your children together, just as a hen gathers her brood under her wings, and you would not have it! Behold, your house is left to you desolate;and I say to you, you will not see Me until the time comes when you say, "BLESSED IS HE WHO COMES IN THE NAME OF THE LORD'" (Lk. 13:31-35)!

They Are Convinced that John Was a Prophet

"On one of the days while He was teaching the people in the temple and preaching the gospel, the chief priests and the scribes with the elders confronted Him, and they spoke, saying to Him, 'Tell us by what authority You are doing these things, or who is the one who gave You this authority?' Jesus answered and said to them, 'I will also ask you a question, and you tell Me: Was the baptism of John from heaven or from men?' They reasoned among themselves, saying, 'If we say, "From heaven," He will say, "Why did you not believe him?" But if we say, "From men," all the people will stone us to death, for they are convinced that John was a prophet.' So they answered that they did not know where it came from. And Jesus said to them, 'Nor will I tell you by what authority I do these things'" (Lk. 20:1-8).

Jesus the Nazarene, Who Was a Prophet Mighty in Deed and Word

"And behold, two of them were going that very day to a village named Emmaus, which was about seven miles from Jerusalem. And they were talking with each other about all these things which had taken place. While they were talking and discussing, Jesus Himself approached and began traveling with them. But their eyes were prevented from recognizing Him. And He said to them, 'What are these words that you are exchanging with one another as you are walking?' And they stood still, looking sad. One of them, named Cleopas, answered and said to Him, 'Are You the only one visiting Jerusalem and unaware of the things which have happened here in these days?' And He said to them, 'What things?' And they said to Him, 'The things about Jesus the Nazarene, who was a prophet mighty in deed and word in the sight of God and all the people, and how the chief priests and our rulers delivered Him to the sentence of death, and crucified Him. But we were hoping that it was He who was going to redeem Israel. Indeed, besides all this, it is the third day since these things happened. But also some women among us amazed us. When they were at the tomb early in the morning, and did not find His body, they came, saying that they had also seen a vision of angels who said that He was alive. Some of those who were with us went to the tomb and found it just exactly as the women also had said; but Him they did not see.' And He said to them, 'O foolish men and slow of heart to believe in all that the prophets have spoken! Was it not necessary for the Christ to suffer these things and to enter into His glory?' Then beginning with Moses and with all the prophets, He explained to them the things concerning Himself in all the Scriptures" (Lk. 24:13-27).

IN THE BOOK OF JOHN

Are You the Prophet?

"This is the testimony of John, when the Jews sent to him priests and Levites from Jerusalem to ask him, 'Who are you?' And he confessed and did not deny, but confessed, 'I am not the Christ.' They asked him, 'What then? Are you Elijah?' And he said, 'I am not.' 'Are you the Prophet?' And he answered, 'No.' Then they said to him, 'Who are you, so that we may give an answer to those who sent us? What do you say about yourself?' He said, 'I am A VOICE OF ONE CRYING IN THE WILDERNESS, "MAKE STRAIGHT THE WAY OF THE LORD," as Isaiah the prophet said'" (Jn. 1:19-23).

You Are Not the Christ, nor Elijah, nor the Prophet

"Now they had been sent from the Pharisees. They asked him, and said to him, 'Why then are you baptizing, if you are not the Christ, nor Elijah, nor the Prophet?' John answered them saying, 'I baptize in water, but among you stands One whom you do not know. It is He who comes after me, the thong of whose sandal I am not worthy to untie.' These things took place in Bethany beyond the Jordan, where John was baptizing" (Jn. 1:24-28).

Sir, I Perceive that You Are a Prophet

"The woman said to Him, 'Sir, give me this water, so I will not be thirsty nor come all the way here to draw.' He said to her, 'Go, call your husband and come here.' The woman answered and said, 'I have no husband.' Jesus said to her, 'You have correctly said, "I have no husband"; for you have had five husbands, and the one whom you now have is not your husband; this you have said truly.' The woman said to Him, 'Sir, I perceive that You are a prophet. Our fathers worshiped in this mountain, and you people say that in Jerusalem is the place where men ought to worship.' Jesus said to her, 'Woman, believe Me, an hour is coming when neither in this mountain nor in Jerusalem will you worship the Father. You worship what you do not know; we worship what we know, for salvation is from the Jews. But an hour is coming, and now is, when the true worshipers will worship the Father in spirit and truth; for such people the Father seeks to be His worshipers. God is spirit, and those who worship Him must worship in spirit and truth.' The woman said to Him, 'I know that Messiah is coming (He who is called Christ); when that One comes, He will declare all things to us.' Jesus said to her, 'I who speak to you am He'" (Jn. 4:15-26).

That a Prophet Has No Honor in His Own Country

"After the two days He went forth from there into Galilee. For Jesus Himself testified that a prophet has no honor in his own country. So when He came to Galilee, the Galileans received Him, having seen all the things that He did in Jerusalem at the feast; for they themselves also went to the feast" (Jn. 4:43-45).

The Prophet Who Is to Come into the World

"After these things Jesus went away to the other side of the Sea of Galilee (or Tiberias). A large crowd followed Him, because they saw the signs which He was performing on those who were sick. Then Jesus went up on the mountain, and there He sat down with His disciples. Now the Passover, the feast of the Jews, was near. Therefore Jesus, lifting up His eyes and seeing that a large crowd was coming to Him, said to Philip, 'Where are we to buy bread, so that these may eat?' This He was saying to test him, for He Himself knew what He was intending to do. Philip answered Him, 'Two hundred denarii worth of bread is not sufficient for them, for everyone to receive a little.' One of His disciples, Andrew, Simon Peter's brother, said to Him, 'There is a lad here who has five barley loaves and two fish, but what are these for so many people?' Jesus said, 'Have the people sit down.' Now there was much grass in the place. So the men sat down, in number about five thousand. Jesus then took the loaves, and having given thanks, He distributed to those who were seated; likewise also of the fish as much as they wanted. When they were filled, He said to His disciples, 'Gather up the leftover fragments so that nothing will be lost.' So they gathered them up, and filled twelve baskets with fragments from the five barley loaves which were left over by those who had eaten. Therefore when the people saw the sign which He had performed, they said, 'This is truly the Prophet who is to come into the world'" (Jn. 6:1-14).

This Certainly Is the Prophet

"'For this is the will of My Father, that everyone who beholds the Son and believes in Him will have eternal life, and I Myself will raise him up on the last day.' Therefore the Jews were grumbling about Him, because He said, 'I am the bread that came down out of heaven.' They were saying, 'Is not this Jesus, the son of Joseph, whose father and mother we know? How does He now say, "I have come down out of heaven"?' Jesus answered and said to them, 'Do not grumble among yourselves. No one can come to Me unless the Father who sent Me draws him; and I will raise him up on the last day'" (Jn. 7:40-44).

No Prophet Arises Out of Galilee

"The officers then came to the chief priests and Pharisees, and they said to them, 'Why did you not bring Him?' The officers answered, 'Never has a man spoken the way this man speaks.' The Pharisees then answered them,

Chapter Three

'You have not also been led astray, have you? No one of the rulers or Pharisees has believed in Him, has he? But this crowd which does not know the Law is accursed.' Nicodemus (he who came to Him before, being one of them) said to them, 'Our Law does not judge a man unless it first hears from him and knows what he is doing, does it?' They answered him, 'You are not also from Galilee, are you? Search, and see that no prophet arises out of Galilee.' Everyone went to his home" (Jn. 7:45-53).

He Is a Prophet

"They brought to the Pharisees the man who was formerly blind. Now it was a Sabbath on the day when Jesus made the clay and opened his eyes. Then the Pharisees also were asking him again how he received his sight. And he said to them, 'He applied clay to my eyes, and I washed, and I see.' Therefore some of the Pharisees were saying, 'This man is not from God, because He does not keep the Sabbath.' But others were saying, 'How can a man who is a sinner perform such signs?' And there was a division among them. So they said to the blind man again, 'What do you say about Him, since He opened your eyes?' And he said, 'He is a prophet'" (Jn. 9:13-17).

That the Word of Isaiah the Prophet Might Be Fulfilled

"Now My soul has become troubled; and what shall I say, 'Father, save Me from this hour'? But for this purpose I came to this hour. 'Father, glorify Your name.' Then a voice came out of heaven: 'I have both glorified it, and will glorify it again.' So the crowd of people who stood by and heard it were saying that it had thundered; others were saying, 'An angel has spoken to Him.' Jesus answered and said, 'This voice has not come for My sake, but for your sakes. Now judgment is upon this world; now the ruler of this world will be cast out. And I, if I am lifted up from the earth, will draw all men to Myself.' But He was saying this to indicate the kind of death by which He was to die. The crowd then answered Him, 'We have heard out of the Law that the Christ is to remain forever; and how can You say, "The Son of Man must be lifted up"? Who is this Son of Man?' So Jesus said to them, 'For a little while longer the Light is among you. Walk while you have the Light, so that darkness will not overtake you; he who walks in the darkness does not know where he goes. While you have the Light, believe in the Light, so that you may become sons of Light.' These things Jesus spoke, and He went away and hid Himself from them. But though He had performed so many signs before them, yet they were not believing in Him. This was to fulfill the word of Isaiah the prophet which he spoke: 'LORD, WHO HAS BELIEVED OUR REPORT? AND TO WHOM HAS THE ARM OF THE LORD BEEN REVEALED?' For this reason they could not believe, for Isaiah said again, 'HE HAS BLINDED THEIR EYES AND HE HARDENED THEIR HEART, SO THAT THEY WOULD NOT SEE WITH THEIR EYES AND PERCEIVE WITH THEIR HEART, AND BE CONVERTED AND I HEAL THEM.' These things Isaiah said because he saw His glory, and he spoke of Him. Nevertheless many even of the rulers believed in Him, but because of the Pharisees they were not confessing Him, for fear that they would be put out of the synagogue; for they loved the approval of men rather than the approval of God" (Jn. 12:27-43).

Chapter Three

IN THE BOOK OF ACTS

This Is What Was Spoken of Through the Prophet Joel

"But Peter, taking his stand with the eleven, raised his voice and declared to them: 'Men of Judea and all you who live in Jerusalem, let this be known to you and give heed to my words. For these men are not drunk, as you suppose, for it is only the third hour of the day; but this is what was spoken of through the prophet Joel: "AND IT SHALL BE IN THE LAST DAYS," God says, "THAT I WILL POUR FORTH OF MY SPIRIT ON ALL MANKIND; AND YOUR SONS AND YOUR DAUGHTERS SHALL PROPHESY, AND YOUR YOUNG MEN SHALL SEE VISIONS, AND YOUR OLD MEN SHALL DREAM DREAMS; EVEN ON MY BONDSLAVES, BOTH MEN AND WOMEN, I WILL IN THOSE DAYS POUR FORTH OF MY SPIRIT And they shall prophesy. AND I WILL GRANT WONDERS IN THE SKY ABOVE AND SIGNS ON THE EARTH BELOW, BLOOD, AND FIRE, AND VAPOR OF SMOKE. 'THE SUN WILL BE TURNED INTO DARKNESS AND THE MOON INTO BLOOD, BEFORE THE GREAT AND GLORIOUS DAY OF THE LORD SHALL COME. AND IT SHALL BE THAT EVERYONE WHO CALLS ON THE NAME OF THE LORD WILL BE SAVED"'" (Ac. 2:14-21).

Because He Was a Prophet

"Brethren, I may confidently say to you regarding the patriarch David that he both died and was buried, and his tomb is with us to this day. And so, because he was a prophet and knew that GOD HAD SWORN TO HIM WITH AN OATH TO SEAT one OF HIS DESCENDANTS ON HIS THRONE, he looked ahead and spoke of the resurrection of the Christ, that HE WAS NEITHER ABANDONED TO HADES, NOR DID His flesh SUFFER DECAY. This Jesus God raised up again, to which we are all witnesses. Therefore having been exalted to the right hand of God, and having received from the Father the promise of the Holy Spirit, He has poured forth this which you both see and hear. For it was not David who ascended into heaven, but he himself says: 'THE LORD SAID TO MY LORD, "SIT AT MY RIGHT HAND, UNTIL I MAKE YOUR ENEMIES A FOOTSTOOL FOR YOUR FEET.'" Therefore let all the house of Israel know for certain that God has made Him both Lord and Christ—this Jesus whom you crucified" (Ac. 2:29-36).

God Shall Raise up for You a Prophet Like Me from Your Brethren

"And now, brethren, I know that you acted in ignorance, just as your rulers did also. But the things which God announced beforehand by the mouth of all the prophets, that His Christ would suffer, He has thus fulfilled. Therefore repent and return, so that your sins may be wiped away, in order that times of refreshing may come from the presence of the Lord; and that He may send Jesus, the Christ appointed for you, whom heaven must receive until the period of restoration of all things about which God spoke by the mouth of His holy prophets from ancient time. Moses said, 'THE LORD GOD WILL RAISE UP FOR YOU A PROPHET LIKE ME FROM YOUR BRETHREN; TO HIM YOU SHALL GIVE HEED to everything He says to you. And it will be that every soul that does not heed that prophet shall be utterly destroyed from among the people.' And likewise, all the prophets who have spoken, from Samuel and his successors onward, also announced these days. It is you who are the sons of the prophets and of the covenant which God made with your fathers, saying to Abraham, 'AND IN YOUR SEED ALL THE FAMILIES OF THE EARTH SHALL BE BLESSED.' For you first, God raised up His Servant and sent Him to bless you by turning every one of you from your wicked ways" (Ac. 3:17-26).

A Prophet Like Me

"This Moses whom they disowned, saying, 'WHO MADE YOU A RULER AND A JUDGE?' is the one whom God sent to be both a ruler and a deliverer with the help of the angel who appeared to him in the thorn bush. This man led them out, performing wonders and signs in the land of Egypt and in the Red Sea and in the wilderness for forty years. This is the Moses who said to the sons of Israel, 'GOD WILL RAISE UP FOR YOU A PROPHET LIKE ME FROM YOUR BRETHREN.' This is the one who was in the congregation in the wilderness together with the angel who was speaking to him on Mount Sinai, and who was with our fathers; and he received living oracles to pass on to you. Our fathers were unwilling to be obedient to him, but repudiated him and in their hearts turned back to Egypt, SAYING TO AARON, 'MAKE FOR US GODS WHO WILL GO BEFORE US; FOR THIS MOSES WHO LED US OUT OF THE LAND OF EGYPT—WE DO NOT KNOW WHAT HAPPENED TO HIM.' At that time they made a calf and brought a sacrifice to the idol, and were rejoicing in the works of their hands. But God turned away and delivered them up to serve the host of heaven; as it is written in the book of the prophets, 'IT WAS NOT TO ME THAT YOU OFFERED VICTIMS AND SACRIFICES FORTY YEARS IN THE WILDERNESS, WAS IT, O HOUSE OF ISRAEL? YOU ALSO TOOK ALONG THE TABERNACLE OF MOLOCH AND THE STAR OF THE

Chapter Three

GOD ROMPHA, THE IMAGES WHICH YOU MADE TO WORSHIP. I ALSO WILL REMOVE YOU BEYOND BABYLON'" (Ac. 7:35-43).

The Most High Does Not Dwell in Houses Made by Human Hands; as the Prophet Says

"Our fathers had the tabernacle of testimony in the wilderness, just as He who spoke to Moses directed him to make it according to the pattern which he had seen. And having received it in their turn, our fathers brought it in with Joshua upon dispossessing the nations whom God drove out before our fathers, until the time of David. David found favor in God's sight, and asked that he might find a dwelling place for the God of Jacob. But it was Solomon who built a house for Him. However, the Most High does not dwell in houses made by human hands; as the prophet says: 'HEAVEN IS MY THRONE, AND EARTH IS THE FOOTSTOOL OF MY FEET; WHAT KIND OF HOUSE WILL YOU BUILD FOR ME?' says the Lord, 'OR WHAT PLACE IS THERE FOR MY REPOSE? WAS IT NOT MY HAND WHICH MADE ALL THESE THINGS" (Ac. 7:44-50)?

He Was Reading the Prophet Isaiah

"So, when they had solemnly testified and spoken the word of the Lord, they started back to Jerusalem, and were preaching the gospel to many villages of the Samaritans. But an angel of the Lord spoke to Philip saying, 'Get up and go south to the road that descends from Jerusalem to Gaza.' (This is a desert road.) So he got up and went; and there was an Ethiopian eunuch, a court official of Candace, queen of the Ethiopians, who was in charge of all her treasure; and he had come to Jerusalem to worship, and he was returning and sitting in his chariot, and was reading the prophet Isaiah. Then the Spirit said to Philip, 'Go up and join this chariot.' Philip ran up and heard him reading Isaiah the prophet, and said, 'Do you understand what you are reading?' And he said, 'Well, how could I, unless someone guides me?' And he invited Philip to come up and sit with him. Now the passage of Scripture which he was reading was this: 'HE WAS LED AS A SHEEP TO SLAUGHTER; AND AS A LAMB BEFORE ITS SHEARER IS SILENT, SO HE DOES NOT OPEN HIS MOUTH. IN HUMILIATION HIS JUDGMENT WAS TAKEN AWAY; WHO WILL RELATE HIS GENERATION? FOR HIS LIFE IS REMOVED FROM THE EARTH.' The eunuch answered Philip and said, 'Please tell me, of whom does the prophet say this? Of himself or of someone else?' Then Philip opened his mouth, and beginning from this Scripture he preached Jesus to him. As they went along the road they came to some water; and the eunuch said, 'Look! Water! What prevents me from being baptized?' [And Philip said, 'If you believe with all your heart, you may.' And he answered and said, 'I believe that Jesus Christ is the Son of God.'] And he ordered the chariot to stop; and they both went down into the water, Philip as well as the eunuch, and he baptized him. When they came up out of the water, the Spirit of the Lord snatched Philip away; and the eunuch no longer saw him, but went on his way rejoicing. But Philip found himself at Azotus, and as he passed through he kept preaching the gospel to all the cities until he came to Caesarea" (Ac. 8:25-40).

A Prophet Named Agabus Came Down from Judea

"When we had finished the voyage from Tyre, we arrived at Ptolemais, and after greeting the brethren, we stayed with them for a day. On the next day we left and came to Caesarea, and entering the house of Philip the evangelist, who was one of the seven, we stayed with him. Now this man had four virgin daughters who were prophetesses. As we were staying there for some days, a prophet named Agabus came down from Judea. And coming to us, he took Paul's belt and bound his own feet and hands, and said, 'This is what the Holy Spirit says: "In this way the Jews at Jerusalem will bind the man who owns this belt and deliver him into the hands of the Gentiles."' When we had heard this, we as well as the local residents began begging him not to go up to Jerusalem. Then Paul answered, 'What are you doing, weeping and breaking my heart? For I am ready not only to be bound, but even to die at Jerusalem for the name of the Lord Jesus.' And since he would not be persuaded, we fell silent, remarking, 'The will of the Lord be done'" (Ac. 21:7-14)!

The Holy Spirit Rightly Spoke through Isaiah the Prophet to Your Fathers

"When they had set a day for Paul, they came to him at his lodging in large numbers; and he was explaining to them by solemnly testifying about the kingdom of God and trying to persuade them concerning Jesus, from both the Law of Moses and from the Prophets, from morning until evening. Some were being persuaded by the things spoken, but others would not believe. And when they did not agree with one another, they began leaving after Paul had spoken one parting word, 'The Holy Spirit rightly spoke through Isaiah the prophet to your fathers, saying, "GO TO THIS PEOPLE AND SAY, 'YOU WILL KEEP ON HEARING, BUT WILL NOT UNDERSTAND; AND YOU WILL KEEP ON SEEING, BUT WILL NOT PERCEIVE; FOR THE HEART OF THIS

Chapter Three

PEOPLE HAS BECOME DULL, AND WITH THEIR EARS THEY SCARCELY HEAR, AND THEY HAVE CLOSED THEIR EYES; OTHERWISE THEY MIGHT SEE WITH THEIR EYES, AND HEAR WITH THEIR EARS, AND UNDERSTAND WITH THEIR HEART AND RETURN, AND I WOULD HEAL THEM.'" Therefore let it be known to you that this salvation of God has been sent to the Gentiles; they will also listen.' [When he had spoken these words, the Jews departed, having a great dispute among themselves]" (Ac. 28:23-29).

IN THE BOOK OF 1 CORINTHIANS

If Anyone Thinks He Is a Prophet or Spiritual

"If anyone thinks he is a prophet or spiritual, let him recognize that the things which I write to you are the Lord's commandment. But if anyone does not recognize this, he is not recognized. Therefore, my brethren, desire earnestly to prophesy, and do not forbid to speak in tongues. But all things must be done properly and in an orderly manner" (1Co. 14:37-40).

IN THE BOOK OF TITUS

A Prophet of Their Own

"For there are many rebellious men, empty talkers and deceivers, especially those of the circumcision, who must be silenced because they are upsetting whole families, teaching things they should not teach for the sake of sordid gain. One of themselves, a prophet of their own, said, 'Cretans are always liars, evil beasts, lazy gluttons.' This testimony is true. For this reason reprove them severely so that they may be sound in the faith, not paying

125

attention to Jewish myths and commandments of men who turn away from the truth. To the pure, all things are pure; but to those who are defiled and unbelieving, nothing is pure, but both their mind and their conscience are defiled. They profess to know God, but by their deeds they deny Him, being detestable and disobedient and worthless for any good deed" (Tit. 1:10-16).

DAILY FAITH CONFESSIONS

(These are not direct quotations from the Bible but are paraphrased confessions based on scripture.)
SAY THEM OUT LOUD.

I am God's child (Jn. 1:12). I am royalty (1 Pet. 2:9). I am hidden with Christ in God (Col. 3:3). I am united with the Lord (1 Cor. 6:17). I am a friend of Christ (Jn. 15:15). I am raised up with Him, and seated with Him in heavenly places in Christ Jesus (Eph. 2:6). I was bought with a price (1 Cor. 6:19-20). I am blessed when I come in, and blessed shall I be when I go out (Deut. 28:6). I am a personal witness of Christ (Acts 1:8). I am a saint who prays in the Holy Spirit to keep myself in the love of God (Jude 1:20-21). I draw near with confidence to the throne of grace (Heb. 4:16). I have been adopted by the Father (Eph. 1:5). I am the salt and light of the earth (Mt. 5:13). I am the head and not the tail, and I am above, and not underneath. I am the lender and not the borrower (Deut. 28:13). I have authority to trample serpents and scorpions and over all the power of the enemy (Lk. 10:19). I am a member of the body of Christ (1 Cor. 12:27). God blessed me to be fruitful, and multiply, and replenish the earth, and subdue it: and have dominion (Gen. 1:28). I cannot be separated from God's love (Ro. 8:39). The good work God has begun in me will be perfected (Phil. 1:5). I can do all things through Christ who strengthens me (Phil. 4:13). No weapon that is formed against me will prosper (Is. 54:17). So then faith cometh by hearing, and hearing by the word of God (Ro. 10:17 KJV). Faith is my currency to operate in the kingdom of God (Ro. 14:23). I am God's workmanship created in Christ Jesus for good works, which God prepared beforehand (Eph. 2:10). I have been appointed to bear fruit, and that my fruit would remain (Jn. 15:16). I am being wise when I am winning souls for King Jesus (Pr. 11:30). My body is the temple of the Holy Spirit (1 Cor. 6:19). I have access to God through the Holy Spirit (Eph. 2:18). I have been justified (Ro. 5:1). Therefore there is now no condemnation for those who are in Christ Jesus (Ro. 8:1). Greater is He who is in me than he who is in the world (1 Jn. 4:4). I will do greater works than Jesus because He went to the Father (Jn. 14:12). As God was with Moses, He will be with me; God will not fail me or forsake me (Jos. 1:5). I see myself the way God see me. God sees me as a king (Gen, 17:6, Rev. 1:6) God sees me as royalty (1 Pet. 2:9). God sees me as the righteousness of God in Christ, bold as a lion (Ro. 3:22, Pr. 28:1). God sees me without spot or wrinkle because of the blood of Jesus (1 Pet. 1:19). I am having faith for big things because God owns everything and I'm His son (Ps. 24:1). No man will be able to stand before me all the days of my life (Jos. 1:5). My Father is glorified by this that I bear much fruit, and proves I'm a disciple (see Jn. 15:8). I think big and confess big things because God is big (Ps. 24:1). I will respect God for the big God that He is and my mouth will create whatever I want (Lk. 6:45). I no longer think of millions, my renewed mind thinks of billions because the wealth of the wicked is laid up for the righteous (Pr. 13:22). The sinner's job is to gather and collect for the one who is good in God's sight (Ecc. 2:26). Redemption is not complete without prosperity. Jesus hung on the cross so I can have the whole package, not just salvation (2 Cor. 8:9). I don't have to qualify, Jesus has qualified me. Jesus reversed the curse. The devil is a liar, and Jesus is the Messiah. Jesus is made unto me wisdom, righteousness, sanctification, and redemption (1 Cor. 1:30). I submit to God, I resist the devil and he flees from me (Jas. 4:7). For God has not given me the spirit of fear; but of power, and of love, and of a sound mind (2 Tim. 1:7). The Holy Spirit will teach me all things (Jn. 14:26). The Holy Spirit will guide me into all truth (Jn.16:13). The Holy Spirit abides in me, and I don't need anyone to teach me, but the anointing teaches me all things (1 Jn. 2:27). I quench fiery darts from the wicked one with the shield of faith (Eph. 6:16). I stand firm against the schemes of the devil (Eph. 6:11). I already have the victory and Satan cannot back me up. I advance and hold. Advance and hold to victory after victory (2 Cor. 2:14). I walk in love and live by faith (Gal. 5:6). I have been redeemed from the curse of the law, poverty, sickness, and spiritual death (Gal. 3:13; Deut. 28). I bear much fruit. I'm God's workmanship created beforehand for good works (Eph. 2:10). God's favor is on my life (Ps. 3:8). God blesses me and His favor surrounds me as with a shield (Ps. 5:12). The kingdom of God is within me (Lk. 17:21). I have a production plant inside of me that bears fruit to change the world (Gen. 1:28). God gives me power to get wealth to establish His covenant on earth (Deut. 8:18). I am blessed to be a blessing (Gen. 12:2). I have Satan on the run and will make a mockery of him (Jas. 4:7). No man will be able to stand before me all the days of my life (Jos. 1:5). God's angels keep me in all my ways (Ps. 91:11).

PRAYER FOR SALVATION

Say the following prayer out loud.

Heavenly Father, I am a sinner and I need a Savior. I confess Jesus Christ as the Lord of my life. I repent of all my sins. Father, I truly believe you raised Jesus from the dead. I pray this prayer in Jesus' name. Father, I am your child because Jesus is my Lord. I want to receive the fullness of the Holy Spirit. Holy Spirit come into me and fill me so I can be a mighty witness for King Jesus. I pray this prayer in Jesus' name. Amen.

PRAYER FOR BAPTISM OF THE HOLY SPIRIT

Say the following prayer out loud.

Father, I am your child because Jesus is my Lord. Jesus said, "How much more shall your heavenly Father give the Holy Spirit to those who ask Him." I ask you now in the name of Jesus to fill me with the Holy Spirit. Thank you, Father, I received the baptism of the Holy Spirit by faith. I yield my vocal organs and expect to speak in tongues as the Holy Spirit gives me utterance in Jesus name. Father, I plan to pray in the Holy Spirit building myself up on my most holy faith, and keep myself in the love of God, as mentioned in Jude 20 and 21. In Jesus name I decree it. Amen.

ABOUT THE AUTHOR

Eugene Carvalho is an administrator, Christian author of seventy-seven books, and the founder of Receiving by Faith. God uses him in the offices of pastor, evangelist and prophet. He holds a bachelor's degree in biblical studies and a double minor in pastoral ministry and world missions. He also holds a master's degree in practical theology. Eugene prayed for a translator and God sent his wife Mercedes who has a six-year degree in Spanish from a university in Tampico, Mexico. They have participated in evangelism in the streets of Mexico for many years. They have also traveled to churches all over the United States and the nation of Mexico winning souls and preaching the gospel of the kingdom. Their website for their ministry is: www.receivingbyfaith.org.

BOOKS BY EUGENE IN ENGLISH

To purchase other books by Eugene Carvalho visit receivingbyfaith.org or amazon.com.

Receiving by Faith
Faith for Every Day: 365 Daily Devotions
Faith Cometh by Hearing, and Hearing by the Word of God
Faith, Hope, and Love
Walk in Love and Live by Faith
Topical Christian Handbook and Scripture Guide
The Gospel Is the Power of God unto Salvation
Seed Time and Harvest Time
Your New Identity in Christ
The Cross and the Blood
The Holy Spirit
The Attributes of God
The Favor of God
The Glory of God
The Grace of God
The Power of God
The Promises of God
The Spirit of God
The Throne of God
The New Testament Church: A Survey from the Book of Ephesians
Vengeance and Recompense
God's Angel's
Prayer and Fasting
God's Mighty Prophets
A Survey of Jesus Through the Epistles

Old Testament Miracles
New Testament Miracles
The Names of Jesus
The Psalms of David
Mountain Moving Confessions
Visions and Dreams
Blessed Beyond Measure
The Righteous Will Flourish like The Palm Tree
Christ Heals: What the Bible Has to Say
My Peace I Give to You
Balancing Grace and Truth
Praise and Worship Changes Everything
Understanding the Importance of Authority
If You Are Willing and Obedient
Have Life More Abundantly
Sing Unto the Lord a New Song
The Power of the Tongue
The Supernatural: What the Bible Has to Say
The Truth Will Make You Free
Joy in the Holy Ghost
Praise Is Powerful: What the Bible Has to Say
Stewardship Regarding Our Finances
Love, Joy, and Peace Are Fruit of the Holy Ghost
Oh, Give Thanks to the Lord for He Is Good
The Kingdom of Heaven is at Hand
Acquiring Wisdom Is Vital
Grace and Mercy: What the Bible Has to Say
God Is Faithful: What the Bible Has to Say
God Is Love: What the Bible Has to Say
The God of Hope: What the Bible Has to Say
Pearls of Wisdom and Gems of Knowledge
Regarding Christianity

Victory is Mine, Joy is Mine, Peace Is Mine: I Told
Satan to Get Thee Behind
The Master's Gems
Striving Toward Perfection
For the Kingdom of God Is Righteousness, Peace
and Joy in the Holy Ghost
Encountering Proverbs, Ecclesiastes, and Song of
Solomon Through a Topical Survey
God's Feasts and Festivals
Speaking the Truth in Love
Spiritual Formation: Unleashing the Kingdom of
God within You
Prayer and Praise: The Big Artillery
Apostles and Prophets: The Foundation of the
Church
Be Strong and Courageous
Covenant: A Concise Survey
Sow Then Reap a Harvest
Grace and Peace Be Multiplied Unto You
Your Word Is a Lamp to Me Feet
Prayer Is Powerful: What the Bible Has to Say
My People Are Destroyed By Lack of Knowledge
God Deserves Pure Worship
The Lord Requires Integrity: The Major Element of
Leadership
A Topical Look at the Book of Deuteronomy
A Topical Look at the Book of Psalms
A Topical Look at the Book of Proverbs
A Topical Look at the Book of Isaiah
A Topical Look at the Book of John
A Topical Look at the Book of Hebrews
A Topical Look at the Book of Revelation

BOOKS BY EUGENE IN SPANISH

Las Promesas de Dios
Los Salmos de David
Lo Sobrenatural: Lo que la Bíblia Tiene que Decir
Una Mirada Topica Del Libro De Los Salmos
Dios es Amor: Lo que la Biblia Tiene que Decir
La Adquisición de la Sabiduría es Vital: Lo que la
Biblia Tiene que Decir

NOTES

NOTES

NOTES